Derek Tangye and his wife ~~left~~ ~~their~~
glamorous life in London when they discovered
Minack, a deserted cottage close to the cliffs of
Mount's Bay in Cornwall. From the wild land
around the cottage they carved the meadows
which became their flower farm and inspired
the Minack Chronicles, the series of bestsellers
which has become famous all over the world.

A *Warner* Book

First published in Great Britain by Michael Joseph Ltd 1990
Published by Sphere Books Ltd 1991
Reprinted by Warner Books 1993
Reprinted 1994, 1996

Printed in England by Clays Ltd, St Ives plc

ISBN 0 7515 0491 2

Warner Books
A Division of
Little, Brown and Company (UK)
Brettenham House
Lancaster Place
London WC2E 7EN

To Alan Brooke

LIST OF ILLUSTRATIONS

Photograph 4 is by Michael Murray/*Woman's Weekly*
6 by Davis Wills
9 by 'the Commando'

I

A quarter to two.

Loggans Mill roundabout was a desolate circle of untidy couch grass. The weather was cold, dismal, snow was threatening. A February day.

I had stopped the Volvo at the side of the roundabout, the Hayle rugby football ground behind me; and from here I could watch the traffic coming up from Hayle town centre, from St Michael's Hospital.

Ten minutes to two.

I stared across to the sand dunes, dreary bungalows dotted among them, and I found myself inconsequently wondering about the people who lived there. Just to keep my mind occupied.

Five minutes to two.

This was the time I was scheduled to meet Jeannie's car, then follow to Truro and beyond to where the service was to be held.

No sign.

Huge fish lorries half circled the roundabout, French names on their sides, Spanish names. Then I saw two familiar lorries, lorries that came from Long Rock near Penzance carrying daffodils to London

and up-country markets, lorries that carried the daffodils that Jeannie used to pick, bunch and box.

I was suffering from a sense of unreality. Could it
be true? Could it possibly be true that my life with
Jeannie was now only a dream? I now belonged to
the great concourse who have experienced the ending
of love. Dante Rossetti's lines went through my mind,
lines I had copied out years ago into my diary, long
before I met Jeannie, as if, mystically, I was preparing
myself for this time.

> As much as in a hundred years she's dead
> Yet it is today the day in which she died.

I sat there and philosophized. I said to myself how
wondrous it was that we had together so many years
of happiness, we who belonged to the borrowed-time
generation. Many of our youthful friends loved,
kissed, said goodbye, promising to meet again . . .
and had been killed in the Hitler war. It is a thought
that has always haunted me. How many of the girls
involved, now elderly, remember that farewell
moment as if it had taken place yesterday? Yes, Jeannie and I had been lucky.

Two o'clock.

I shifted in my seat, grew into a panic. Had I
missed the car, and it had gone on without me?
Surely it would have been punctual?

Opposite, on the other side of the roundabout, was
the vast yellow and blue building of a Pickfords
transport depot. I would go there, I decided, and ask
to borrow the telephone.

I entered the small office, a girl at a desk, a tall

2

man in green overalls talking to her, telling her of the journey he had made in his lorry from Manchester. I stood listening to them, not believing the question I had to ask of the girl. The man droned on, and I interrupted.

'Excuse me,' I said, and I heard my voice sounding absurdly shy, 'could I use your telephone? You see, it is my wife's funeral, and I was going to meet her at the roundabout, and she is late.'

I remember there was no emotional reaction from either the girl or the man. I might have been talking about the weather. Just a matter-of-fact reply: 'Please do,' handing me the telephone.

So many flowers, I was to learn, had delayed the departure. So many flowers to arrange, including the sheaf of golden daffodils I had picked myself from the meadows down Minack cliff, edging the sea. The car should be at the roundabout any minute, I was told; and it was.

I was glad I was alone. Conventional arrangements had been suggested – a procession of cars, close family accompanying me. What would we have talked about? How could I have separated myself from their well-meaning attitudes? I needed no support. I wanted to be alone with Jeannie on the way to Truro and beyond.

We travelled along the new by-pass, which meant we cut out the road Jeannie and I had used over the years on our journeys towards the River Tamar and London. There was a pub on that old road at Connor Downs where we had the celebration lunch for the publication of *A Cat in the Window*, Jeannie's mother playing the hostess; and a month before that occasion we had stopped at the same pub with Penny, our newly acquired donkey, in the well of the Land-rover, a black donkey who had been born in the Connemara Hills of Ireland.

'Good heavens,' said the publican as we drew up, Penny's head resting on my shoulder as I sat in the driving seat, 'I never expected a donkey to be a customer!'

The by-pass avoided Connor Downs, avoided Roseworthy Hill, once the most obstinate bottleneck in West Cornwall; it careered its way instead through undulating farmland, skirting the towns of Camborne and Redruth. As I now travelled along it alone, a few yards behind Jeannie's car, other cars passing us in the outside lane, my mind was full of Jeannie . . . remembering.

I remembered the first glance she gave me. An air raid was in progress, the windows of the River Room at the Savoy Hotel were boarded up to prevent bomb blast, Carroll Gibbon and his orchestra were playing 'A Nightingale Sang in Berkeley Square', uniforms clung together on the dance floor; and a few yards away from my table sat Jeannie, a naval officer at her side. The alertness of her glance is with me for ever.

I remembered the way she used to run across Richmond Green on a Sunday. I lived then at Cholmondley House, overlooking the river, at the bottom of Friars Lane, and on a Sunday there was always a lunch gathering of journalists, politicians, foreign diplomats and other interesting people visiting London. We were not married then. Jeannie was still

4

living at St Albans with her parents, but every Sunday she left her St Albans home to act as my hostess at the gathering. I would walk to meet her train but I was always late. Hence I would see her in the distance on Richmond Green, and she would be running towards me, a gazelle. It was a signal of her infectious enthusiasm for life.

My mother described her as a pocket Venus. She was five feet five inches tall, with dark hair to her shoulders, a twenty-two-inch waist, slim legs, a mischievous smile and a voice which captured me and many others. I would ask her to go on talking just to listen to her voice, and her voice on the telephone was bewitching. Danny Kaye, who wrote the foreword to her classic *Meet Me at the Savoy*, was also bewitched, though he also used to make jokes about it, mimicking it because of its contrast with the American twang. Indeed he sang a song in the *The Secret Life of Walter Mitty* based on her voice; and amusingly he called the song 'Pamela'. And now here I was at the wheel of the car, travelling behind her, remembering her voice. She had a teasing way of using it, especially on the telephone. 'Hello, hello, hello,' she would softly say when ringing me from Room 205, her Savoy office. Then adding: 'Me here.'

I remembered her watching me, the cat-hater, when introducing me to the ginger kitten playing with a typewriter ribbon on her office carpet, the kitten who was to become Monty of *A Cat in the Window*. How would I react? We had been married three months. A crucial moment in a new marriage. Would she win this early challenge? And she did of course.

5

I remembered the contrariness in her nature. One moment the sophisticated hostess at a Savoy or Claridge's restaurant table, the next a child-like innocence.

One such example occurred on the day Roy Plomley invited me to be a Desert Island Castaway. We lunched beforehand at Claridge's, Derek Drescher the programme producer coming too. At lunch Jeannie was in her customary role, the sophisticated hostess, but after the lunch was over she was child-like. We were about to set off for the studio when Jeannie started saying goodbye.

Roy looked at her. 'Aren't you coming with us?' he said. 'We're waiting for you.'

'Oh,' she replied, 'I didn't think you would want me.'

Jeannie won her victories by femininity, not feminism. Femininity is a subtle weapon, feminism a blunt one. Jeannie won victories against male chauvinism by charm, patience, sex appeal, ability. At the Savoy where she guided the publicity and public relations efforts of the whole Savoy company, she was in a male-dominated world but she never complained that her sex was at a business disadvantage. Indeed she found her femininity the ingredient of her success.

I remembered how decisively she made up her mind to leave her glamorous job when her career was at its height, when the chairman of the Savoy offered her six months' paid holiday, adding: 'You'll be longing to come back before then.' In retrospect I realize how I took her attitude for granted. I was so sure that we were as one that I did not have to fear her attitude was a temporary enthusiasm; and a few months later, after we had settled in the cottage, I was tested in the same kind of fashion. A contract was offered me to write the biography of the legendary Gertrude Lawrence. Gertrude Lawrence herself had chosen me to do it; and the lure included travelling to New York and Hollywood. I had no hesitation in turning it down. We both *knew* our destiny lay at Minack.

I remembered the early years when we had no electricity, no running water, the water coming from the little stream or from the water butt, and the cooking carried out on a Primus stove or a paraffin-heated oven. A bath, in winter, was a hip bath, a rock pool on summer days. Lighting in the cottage came from Tilley lamps (why were they called Tilley?) and when dusk was falling Jeannie would tell me it was time to light them, and I would go through the routine of taking the clasp out of its jar containing methylated spirit, fixing the clasp beneath the comb of the Tilley lamp, putting a match to it, then waiting for it to heat the comb. Once it was heated I started to use the pump on the Tilley, and within a minute or two there was a bright light, provided by the paraffin in the well of the lamp. The smell of the methylated spirit and the paraffin I remember most. It was so basically primitive, such a contrast to the world we had left. Nothing false. We had joined those who had lived in the cottage in times past.

I remembered fragments of her life ... dressed in a yellow oiler picking Governor Herrick violets in pouring rain, picking early February daffodils in the small meadows close to the sea ... her hands in the soil picking up new potatoes ... walking across a field, a jug of tea in each hand, catering for the helpers who were with us at the height of the potato season ... holding a dazed peregrine falcon in her hand which had nose-dived into the garden chasing a dunnock ... holding Monty in her arms, holding Lama, holding Oliver, holding Ambrose, holding Cherry ... carrying Fred the baby donkey into the stables after Penny had given birth to him in the field through which now runs the coastal path ...

The brown bread she baked ... the lovely smile she always gave to strangers who might call at the door ... Provocative moments when in London I had not been able to contact her during the day: 'Where have you been, who with?' Answer: 'Why should I tell you?' – always excitement with her, always a love affair kept alight by the unexpected ...

Watching her concentrate on a drawing of one of the cats, a drawing which would be an illustration for one of my books, a drawing which made you *feel* the cat ... and other drawings which were for sale which she was never confident enough to sell at their true value ... Thinking of the time when her first novel *Hotel Regina*, later to become a bestseller, was turned down in strong terms both by a literary agent and a publisher, and how we wondered why they had to be so vicious about it ... Thinking of the hut in the wood where she wrote it, and how I led her there after the rejection letters had been received, having left a bottle of champagne outside it with a note: 'Bugger them all!' ...

Jeannie entertaining in the cottage, cooking, talking to the guests, never making them feel embarrassed by

the effort she was making, the natural hostess . . .
Then there was the touchy Jeannie: she returned
from shopping one day, indignantly saying a shopkeeper had accused her of not paying for her previous
week's bill, and he said so in front of customers, and
she never went into the shop again . . . There was the
generous Jeannie who, when she gave a present,
measured the person's character by the time taken in
thanking her . . . I remembered the scene of Fred's
birthday party, Fred the donkey, with Jeannie beside
the birthday cake, the children laughing around her
and Fred . . .

Long before that we were staying at a farm at
Mevagissey, and we went for long walks around the
area, and one day we went to Fowey, then off to find
Menabilly which Daphne du Maurier had made im-
mortal in *Rebecca*. Soon Daphne was to occupy it,
renew it, but when Jeannie and I first saw it, the
ancient stone walls were clad in ivy, the house
deserted, and we felt we belonged to the era of
the novel . . . That same day I suddenly suggested
we should visit an old friend of my mother's, Mrs
Treffry, a legendary Fowey family name. Jeannie
looked at me in astonishment: 'We can't go with you
looking like that. You haven't got a tie!' . . .

The day Merlin came to Minack, let out of a
horsebox at the top of the lane by the farm, then
charging down the lane as if he knew he was coming
home, Jeannie clinging to the rein as Merlin jumped
Monty's Leap, sped past the stable building, then to
the gate where Fred was waiting . . . Jeannie finding
Cherry at the base of the cherry tree . . .

Her courage over the years . . . her courage when

she set off for the hospital, blowing kisses as she left, and calling out: 'I love Minack! I love Minack!'

We had reached the outskirts of Truro, and I began to worry about myself. How would I behave? Here I was at the second giant moment of my life, first the wedding day, now the ending day. How would I behave?

We passed the roundabout which, if we had turned right, would have led to Lambe Creek where Jeannie and I spent our first holiday together; and to Rose Cottage where I once lived alone, except for my Old English Sheepdog Roy, writing the first chapters of *Time Was Mine*, and from where, one Saturday afternoon, I went to join up in the Duke of Cornwall's Light Infantry.

Then down the hill of the Truro circular road, passing the turning to the Farm Industries building which we used regularly to visit for practical reasons; and then on to another roundabout where again there was a turning we took for practical reasons: up a hill was the nursery where we used to collect every late March three thousand Maascross tomato plants.

Now up Tregolls Road we went, a route of nostalgic youthful memories because my father and mother used to meet me at Truro station at the beginning of school holidays, Gay the Maltese terrier, Lance, then Roy, the Old English Sheepdogs, barking their welcome, still barking as we drove up Tregolls Road. And at the top of the hill we turned left towards Newquay and my home of Glendorgal. I became again my youthful self in mind as we now turned that corner.

Familiar faces greeted me at the entrance to the chapel. I had not expected them to trouble. Two special friends from London had had their rail journey interrupted by a cliff fall on to the railway line at Dawlish, but they were there. I was very touched by all who had come, and I knew I now had the strength to help me win.

II

I am sitting on the sofa, Ambrose purring on my lap, and I have been talking to him, seeking reassurance that all went well. I don't think I did anything, or said anything, I shouldn't have done. At the end of the service I stood at the entrance to the chapel, shaking hands with those who had come, thanking them. I was in a daze and I do not remember the faces.

The evening gull was here on the roof as dusk fell, still and silent as usual. Why does he only come at dusk? A strange sentinel. Merlin was by the stable gate, and Ambrose had come to me from the far end of the room when I unlatched the door. No sign of Cherry as yet.

How Jeannie would have warmed to Canon Cotter, Vicar of Zennor, a Franciscan, who took the service. I tried hard to keep back my tears when he gently said, as Jeannie slipped away, that the organist would play the Tara theme from *Gone with the Wind*. I had chosen it because Jeannie had the same passion for Minack as

Scarlett O'Hara had for Tara. How lovely it was.

Everyone was deeply moved by David's* address, beautifully delivered, and the contents so sensitively reflecting Jeannie's character. I was so touched by it and I am thinking back to three mornings ago when he brought me a handwritten copy of what he intended to say, shyly, saying that I could change anything if I wanted to; he left it with me, then went outside the cottage, just as I used to do when leaving Jeannie to read a new chapter of a book. I would go out, walk up to the bridge and wait nervously for her reaction. How exultant was the moment when she was enthusiastic! And how exultant was the moment after I had read what David had written.

He told me he had written it in the dawn hours, then had gone out for a walk along the cliffs; and when he had returned he had been amazed to find a robin on his desk. He had never seen a robin in his house before.

A robin was Jeannie's emblem, in that a robin had always played a mystical part in our lives at Minack. The first friends I went to after Jeannie had died were John Miller, the famous artist, and Michael Truscott, picture framer and restorer. They live at Sancreed. They gave me all the possible comfort that true friends can give. When I was leaving, John and I spent several minutes talking as I sat at the wheel of the Volvo outside the house, and the door of the car was open . . .

* David Cornwell (John Le Carré).

I said goodbye to John, moved off, turned left outside the entrance when a robin suddenly appeared, settling on my shoulder. I stopped the car, opened the window beside me, and after a few seconds, still on my shoulder, it flew out, settling on a branch on the other side of the road. A few moments later it began warbling a song. Why did that robin not fly away when the car door was open and I was talking to John? Why did a robin sit on David's desk?

Cherry has just come in, little black Cherry. Her back is to me, she is eating a saucer of lemon sole which I had meant specially for Ambrose. He is still purring, but he is watching her.

In a time of great distress one requires more from a friend than one should ever reasonably expect of that friend. There is a great solace for one's personal sadness, therefore, when that hope is fulfilled. I will always remember with everlasting gratitude David saying to me that those at the service will feel flat afterwards, and that he and Jane, if I agreed, planned to have drinks and food for all those who would like to come to their house afterwards. 'There may be only a dozen or maybe a hundred,' he said. 'We don't know but we will be ready.' So very generous. As it happens there were over a hundred.

I am sitting here wanting to read the address again, but Ambrose is still on my lap and I don't want to move him, and the copy of the address is on my desk. I feel very cool. My emotions are under control, or are they? I have been behaving like an experienced actor, hiding my true self, playing a part I was forced to play. Anytime now I will be myself again, and then . . .

Good, Ambrose has jumped off my lap, gone to see whether Cherry has left any of the lemon sole. I can now fetch the copy of the address.

David Cornwell's Address

Some people die and we feel we hardly knew them.

Some people die and if we were honest we would be hard put to know why they had lived at all.

And some people die leaving us with a sense of reproach: 'If only I'd been nicer to her. If I'd only managed to let him know I liked him.'

Jean Nicol Tangye, the heroine of the Minack Chronicles, was none of these people. She died in the full knowledge of our love, and we shall continue to live in the full knowledge of hers. We need reproach ourselves with nothing. And the best thing we can do, as we meet here now to honour her and mourn her, is to give her from our hearts the collective evidence of our love. Of our joy. And of our luck in knowing her.

Jeannie was a woman faultlessly of her period.

All her life she belonged to the glitter, the drama, the heroism and the sacrifice of her time.

She might have died in the war. She knew an awful lot of people who did. Flying bombs nearly killed her three times. But Jeannie was tough as well as beautiful, and she took a lot of killing.

All her life, it seemed to me, Jeannie wore the unmistakable, almost Churchillian air of a beautiful, well-bred English girl who was ready any time to hop into a siren suit and do some perfectly filthy job. All her life she remained ready to roll up her sleeves for her friends, who included the animals, for whom she had a magic touch, and the countless readers, fans and odd bodies for whom she always had the time.

And when she wasn't killed, she embraced wholeheartedly the obligations of a survivor.

So did Derek. 'A war had come and gone,' he wrote, 'and I had survived and every day of my life I was grateful. Awareness of the luck came to me in sudden moments, reminding me I was one of those who lived on borrowed time.'

Jeannie too remained supremely loyal to her luck. And to her duty towards those who hadn't shared it.

She lived with a determination to make every hour pay. And she did every hour proud. With a courage that was as true to her as she was to life. With straightness, wit and superb style, all the way. Not a nurse in the hospital who, passing her bed, did not pause for a smile of affirmation from Jeannie's clear farseeing eyes. Just as we, in better times, came to expect her smile as of right.

And by living so fully, Jeannie kept all her magical variety alive.

She got extra years – hundreds of extra years – for being so many people; to Derek, and to us.

The champagne girl. The Savoy girl. The girl about town, with a distinctly modern way of selecting her pleasures.

The shrewdie, and the rogue.

She was both private and gregarious.

She could bubble away for hours. Or she could share with you the solid companionship of silence, and let the cliff do the talking.

She was frail, feminine and giddy. She was industrious, conscientious and rock-like under pressure.

She could be totally unheeding of convention. But she knew the rules.

She was a child and died a child. She cared for her looks and never lost them. She was Cecil Beaton's girl on her deathbed.

But above all Jeannie knew men and led us brilliantly from behind, as Derek must know better than all of us together.

She gave us our stature.

She knew the precariousness of our male pride. She inspired forward instincts in us.

And when we were down, when we were being impossible, and moody, and argumentative, she willed us gently back into line, determined never to break the precious membrane between aggression and despair.

A smile and a word and a drink with Jeannie and your writer's block had crumbled at her feet. To walk over the cliff, to take Jeannie and Derek away from their daffodils and share a bottle with them and look across a blue sea to the Lizard was a renewal of the eyes and heart, a renewal of the sheer fun of being alive that every one of us here, thanks to Jeannie, has experienced.

Jeannie was a distinguished writer. In *Hotel Regina*, in *Home is the Hotel*, in *Bertioni's Hotel*, and in the legendary *Meet Me at the Savoy*, she showed us how she could synthesize experience, spin a tale and mingle manners with reality. And there was the artist Jeannie, brilliantly simple and evocative.

But in order to help Derek create, she sublimated her own creative talents. For her love required that Derek himself, and the many thousands who looked to him for nourishment and guidance, should be the greatest of her creations.

And love itself is the real body of work that she has left behind. In her friendships, in her triumphant marriage, that unending love story which Derek has celebrated in the Chronicles.

Jeannie and Derek have taught a lot of people how to live. And now Jeannie has taught us how to live on.

1 March

My birthday, and I am thinking how I used to madden Jeannie because, as I was born in a Leap Year, I would change the dates. Sometimes I would say I wanted my birthday on the 28th, sometimes 1 March ... and then to be thoroughly perverse, having had it on the 28th, I'd say I wanted another on the 1st. Yet I hate birthdays. It seems so unnecessary to be reminded that time is passing. Nonetheless I will now celebrate with Jeannie because it will bring her close. I will bring out the yellow cut glass which was her special one, and the one she gave me, and I will open a bottle of Moet.

In the evening: I went into Penzance this morning, and collected the cards containing the names of all those who sent flowers for Jeannie, and then I copied them on the copier. And I also got copies of *The Times* in which there was a wonderful tribute to Jeannie by Sir Hugh Wontner, chairman of the Savoy Hotel company. How Jeannie would be pleased! She held Sir Hugh in such high regard. The doyen of world hoteliers, the man whose taste and style has maintained the standards of the Savoy Hotel company over so many years.

But now it is evening, the Moet bubbles have gone and I am feeling sad. Never once did she ever think she was going to die. Soon it will begin to dawn on me that I now will always be on my own. But the most wonderful letters are arriving to comfort me.

2 March

I stayed in bed till twelve, Ambrose curled up beside me. So many are saying they are praying for me. So kind but what can be obtained? If the prayers are answered and I am consoled, and go about my normal business, the prayers have taken away my adoration for Jeannie, making me appear casual in my love. There are so many contrary factors to work out. I am confused. Yet I sense the prayers are helping to soothe me.

The only way to survive at the moment is not to think, not to remember, but to shut my eyes to echoes around the cottage in the form of scent bottles, face cream, shoes, the red coat which was my favourite. Today is a day of trying to forget. Tomorrow letter answering must begin. And, in practical terms, what am I planning to eat?

4 March

I had the idea of her memorial service in the last day or two of her life. It was agony witnessing her brave, hopeful smile when there I was beside her thinking how she could be remembered.

My idea was not to have an ordinary memorial service. For Jeannie I had the idea that her memorial service on the chosen day could be held anywhere in the world, at any time, at any place convenient for anyone wishing to join in. Hence someone might be in a bus in London, or in an office in New York, or in a plane flying to New Zealand or Australia, or in a traffic jam in Toronto, or just locally in a field. The date I have chosen is 23 March, her birthday; and so I am sending out cards to those who write, and in due course I will put it in *The Times* and the *Telegraph*. Here is what I am saying:

Those who knew Jean Nicol Tangye in her
Savoy Hotel, Claridge's and Berkeley world, and
those who knew her as the heroine of the Minack
Chronicles, are invited to join together in remembering her, sometime during Sunday 23
March, and wherever they may be ... placing
the Cornish daffodil meadows in their minds
which she loved so much, as the setting of her
Memorial Service.

The daffodils which, over the years, we picked
for market, are in profusion everywhere. I will
not be able to pick them this year and, since I do
not mind being called a sentimental fool, I am
sure the daffodils themselves are delighted. So
much more pleasant to spend their lives on a
Cornish cliff, than a period in a town flower
shop, a time in a vase, and ending in a dustbin.

5 March

Oh, such wonderful letters from total strangers ... 'I only knew her through the books
but I feel I have lost a very dear friend,' is said
over and over again. And there are the words of
consolation, 'You will have so many happy
memories.' I have often written such words of
consolation to people myself, but now that they
are addressed to me I find they make me sad
instead of soothing me. The very fact they were
happy and now can never be shared brings on
the tears. She looked like a child when I last saw

her in her hospital bed. There was no sign of illness, just a hint of her lovely smile. Why did she have to die? There must have been a purpose in her dying. Time will show what it is.

6 March

Panic. I woke up in the middle of the night, realizing I still had not found my gold wrist-watch, the watch which is so precious to me because she gave it to me the year *The Way to Minack* was published, and she had a special inscription put on the back. I am bewildered by my behaviour because I have not made a serious search for it, thinking that it would just turn up; and it hasn't. I couldn't find it on the Monday before the funeral, and I had so wanted it to be with me. I just have to blame all that has been going on as to why I haven't done anything. Now I am about to make a real search . . .

. . . Two hours later and not a sign. I've gone through every cupboard, unravelled every piece of paper, looked under the beds, gone through my clothes, searched every part of the spare room. I am very upset.

7 March

I've done something practical today. I've planted out the Fortune lettuce I sowed in January ('I'm looking forward to these,' Jeannie had said), and a row of the delicious Foremost early potatoes, and a packet of old-fashioned scented sweet peas in pots, all in the Orlyt green-house.

I had spring cabbage, mashed potatoes and sausages for supper. Looked again for the watch. No sign.

8 March

Why has Cherry started to be a thief? A couple of nights ago she grabbed a piece of meat in the kitchen. Yesterday I found her on the dresser trying to unscramble the foil which wrapped my sausages. Ambrose has never been a thief, or has he, and I have forgotten? He is making such a very great fuss of me, as if he knows that he is now my closest friend. Last night he snuggled up on my pillow, occasionally licked my face, purred, made little yapping noises, pinioning me so that I could not move for fear of offending the love he was showing me.

This evening I felt *very* strongly that I should get a companion for Merlin, as if Jeannie was willing me to do so. Over a year since Fred died, and then there was the strange episode of Nellie, Nellie the donkey of the neighbouring farm with whom he had a frustrating love affair . . . and for whom he made the incredible journey when she was dying, undoing the two Minack gates, walking the mile-long lane, turning right towards the neighbouring farm, turning right again towards the entrance . . . he had never been there before. Only his instinct led him. He is a very sensitive donkey.

I have an address to write to, but, being a Pisces, I am hesitating.

10 March

I was having a down day until Joan and Ron arrived at tea-time with a cake. It was my fault. I was feeling miserable and proceeded to make myself more miserable by playing on the record player songs like 'These Foolish Things', 'This is my Lovely Day', 'We'll Gather Lilacs', 'A Nightingale Sang in Berkeley Square' . . .

But Joan and Ron brightened me up. They have been such a wonderful support these past few weeks. Joan not only coming on Monday as usual to clear up the week's mess, but voluntarily coming in other days. Strange that by reading *A Gull on the Roof* during her lunch hour in London where she was a secretary that they decided to leave London for Cornwall, and now are helping me when I most need help. We began laughing at her account in *The Cherry Tree* when she looked after Minack while we paid a London visit, and how she lost her nerve when she was with the donkeys. Her mother died last summer, and she said: 'I find the sadness suddenly comes in waves, bringing tears.' I replied: 'Yes, in sudden waves.'

12 March

Watch found!

I had taken the dustbins up to the farm collecting point before breakfast, and I saw Jack, then Walter whom I used to call the Pied Piper of cats because he had so many, but now he has only one. Jack was very gentle, saying he hadn't known what to do, come and see me, or leave me alone. And I said I was fine, that I would carry on as always, and that Minack had this soothing quality which helped to make me feel at ease. Walter, eighty years old but happy doing the work of a young labourer, held out his hand to me, and there were tears: 'I loved her, you know.' Then he added: 'She looked so young, so very young.'

I opened a tin of sliced peaches for breakfast, then went into the spare room. I had been asking Jeannie for days to help me find the watch, one of those comforting questions which, truthfully, one doesn't expect to be answered. It is a form of emotional lifebelt. Anyhow here is what happened.

For the past two nights Ambrose has deserted me, sleeping on the bed in the spare room, at the end by the door and the bedside table. It was an area which Joan and I had searched dozens of times. Ambrose, however, I was to remember, did come to my bed in the early hours of this morning, yapping, waking me up for a while, then he jumped off my bed and went elsewhere.

Nothing strange about that; but when, after my sliced peaches, I went into the spare room I found, exactly where Ambrose had been sleeping . . . the watch!

15 March

I found a champagne cork in her purse, and in it was stuck a sixpenny piece, a gesture for good luck. What had been the cause for celebration?

17 March

Sudden echoes of her tantalizing voice: 'People, people ...' as she heard someone coming up the path.

'Hello my presh!' (to Ambrose).

'Oh how lucky we are, how lucky!'

'I'll be all right in a moment, I'll be all right ... don't fuss me!'

'Paint the bedroom windows, and I'll be back in two days, and the smell will have gone.'

18 March

I am living with a fantasy. Go back to the finding of the watch for instance. I had said to my fantasy Jeannie that if she was really with me, could she prove it by finding the watch? And she did. Ambrose hadn't slept on the spare bed close to the little table for years, and there it was just where he had curled. And we had searched the bed any number of times. If only I could touch my fantasy.

And I have been thinking of the Hatchards' party which we should have been at. I visioned her in the dress she had specially bought for the occasion but which I knew at the time she would never wear. I imagined the two of us in the Martini Terrace room at the top of New Zealand House in the Haymarket, standing by the long window, staring out over the roofs of London. But I had to stop my thoughts, and think instead what I could have for supper. Sardines would be simple, with buttered toast.

19 March

Today I have made the big decision. I started off by going on a walk with Merlin around Oliver land before I had breakfast. It was a lovely soft spring morning, and we went up the side of the field to the blackthorn alley, then along it, and along the track where gorse on the left of it is advancing year by year, reminding me of a vast, demonstrating mob; and on the right are the badger setts, and I realized that at the very moment of our passing newly born cubs were sleeping deep below us. We reached the Ambrose Rock, and I sat on it, pondering; and Merlin grazed a few feet away, delighted to find a clump or two of tasty campion. I sat there looking back at the cottage, or at the blue expanse of sea, or at the celandines around my feet. I was in no hurry. Time was mine.

Merlin began moving away, and I followed him; and we went to the far end of Oliver land, then round to the right as if we were aiming for Carn Barges but, because of nature's barbed wire in the form of undergrowth and brambles, there was no way to reach Carn Barges. Oliver land is surrounded by nature's barbed wire, and so the busy bodies who walk the countryside looking for opportunities to make trouble are thwarted. Only those who seek the peace of solitude, who seek the *real* naturalness of the countryside, are welcome.

Daffodils were yellow in long disused meadows. Daffodils which at one time were

fashionable and much sought-after; and as I
passed them, their stems struggling through the
winter undergrowth, I pondered about the super-
ficiality of fashion, and those who dictate it.
Boardrooms dictate it. The need for novelty
dominates it. The media is brainwashed to brain-
wash the public.

Merlin and I went back by the honeysuckle
meadow, and I paused there thinking how neat-
minded people might disapprove of the way I
have left the ground where Jeannie's ashes lie.
Nothing organized about it because Jeannie
wanted it like that. Everything natural around
her, wild grasses, sorrel, celandines, wild so-
called weeds which I do not know the name of,
though today there were also to be seen the
snowdrops on the bank behind the shaky white
seat, snowdrops which came from St Cadix,
home of our friend Raleigh Trevelyan, snowdrops which Jeannie had dug for herself one
visit; and there were Bournemouth Gem violets
in contrast among them, and there was a clump
of burgeoning primroses in front of the seat, and
scented stems of three soleil d'or.

Merlin had gone off on his own and, after a
period of contemplation, I followed him . . .
along the track back to the big field which, in
past times, was known as the clover field; and
when I reached it, Merlin was waiting for me,
and it was at that moment my decision was
made.

I returned to the cottage, wrote out a cheque
for £50, and despatched it by the postman who

came with the mail, to the lady who was wanting to sell a donkey called Susie at St Tudy, near Bodmin.

When I handed the envelope to Mike, the postman, he broke into a smile, yet also there was a stillness about him. 'Oh,' he said, 'she would like that, she would like that very much.' And he was thinking of Jeannie.

20 March

'You'll find long winter nights are the torment,' said a letter. 'Inner strength will bring you through,' said another.

And as the letters pour in, I think of all the trouble the writers have taken. I think of them worrying as to what to say, re-writing the letter to get it right, addressing the envelope, posting it ... none of these things are done without much effort. And now, foolishly probably, I am myself worrying about replying and thanking, and how I will find the time and the words to say how profoundly I appreciate the letters which give me much comfort.

21 March

No reply yet from the St Tudy lady about Susie. I had asked if she could be brought here on Wednesday. I trust there will be no change of mind. Susie, I am told, is a little grey donkey, She is five years old and, I am assured, very lovable.

22 March

Despite it being Saturday Ron brought Joan

here this morning, and there is a major clean-up going on in readiness for the memorial service tomorrow afternoon. Only a few people will be coming in person, but from the letters I know there will be people all over the world thinking of her at some time during the day. I have been picking daffodils, filling the cottage and the porch with them; and just now the Penzance florist has delivered a beautiful bouquet of iris, tulips and daffodils sent by a Toronto reader who had visited us, with a note: 'We will be thinking of Jeannie on the 23rd.' And there was a letter from Christchurch, New Zealand: 'Our church is having a minute's silence for Jeannie.'

Joan is now sponging down the walls, and I have the task of putting order to the top of my desk and of sorting all the papers and files which litter the sofa, the porch and the main armchair. What is the gift which makes some people so neat? I have no such gift, nor had Jeannie. I go through letters, newspapers, bills, placing them in files but at the end of the day my desk is untidy as ever. So many things that I *might* want I leave on my desk. Of course there is the easy way out, and that is to bundle everything in empty cardboard wine cases, and hide them in the corner where the gramophone records are stored. Needless to say I always forget what were the things I stored away, and time-wasting searching will occur in due course.

Thank goodness all is well about Susie. She is going to arrive in a horsebox around midday on Wednesday.

An odd thing happened this morning. I went into Jeannie's studio for a sit-down and a think. I looked around at her unfinished pictures, at the paintbrushes untouched since she touched them, at the reference books she had gathered to help her with her hotel novels, at the Zeiss binoculars I had given her, at the photograph of her father in the officer uniform of the London Scottish, at a painting we have never hung on a wall of the view of the Thames opposite Cholmondley House in Richmond where we had our wedding reception . . . and at her schoolgirl desk. It was in a slot of that desk where I found the lines she had written when Penny had died and which she had never shown me:

> The spirits of Minack
> Welcome you
> To their world of Forever
> Where life continues
> And death is never.

The odd thing which had happened occurred when I went out of the studio on to the grass of the stable field. There in front of me was a sick rabbit. I haven't seen a sick rabbit for ages, and the sight of it unnerved me because one of the silly names I often called Jeannie was Bunny.

The service was very simple and intensely moving. The weather was cold and windy, and not the ideal weather for the occasion. But there were daffodils galore and we stood among them, Merlin too, as we listened to Canon Cotter saying a few words, then reading a passage from Corinthians. The backdrop was the rough sea of Mount's Bay, white horses rushing in the wake of the wind, and the line of the Lizard in the distance. I held Merlin on a halter, and he was very submissive, as if he was aware that this was an important occasion. Then, when it was over, I released him from his halter as a reward and, after a second's hesitation, off he danced, kicking his back hooves in delight, scattering, I fear, a few heads of the Joseph McLeod daffodils.

Strange that I should have received a cable this morning from the Australian girl who had helped to plant the bulbs of those daffodils. The cable read: 'I cry for you. Love Fran.'

Fran had been on a world tour, and for a season she helped us, and we have never lost touch. Her arrival here had coincided with our investment in a large number of these Joseph McLeod daffodils which are of a deep yellow and are long-lasting in a vase.

Joseph McLeod was a wartime BBC announcer, and the breeder of the bulb was a Dutchman living in Amsterdam. One night, the seedling of the bulb on the mantlepiece, he was listening secretly to the BBC, when he heard the Gestapo outside. He hid his radio set, and waited. Soon he realized he was not going to be discovered, and he turned on the radio again. He just caught the end of the News ... 'And this was Joseph McLeod reading it.' 'Ah,' the Dutch-man said, 'that will be the name of my seedling.'

When the afternoon was over, and I was alone again, I sat for a while on the sofa staring vacantly into space. Then the wind began to drop, a silence around the cottage. I decided I needed mystical company, and if I were to find such company, I would most likely do so on the bridge where Jeannie and I had spent so much time together; and just a few feet above the hedge behind us on the bridge, is the Lama field, where the memorial service had been held.

I had been standing there for a few minutes when Ambrose suddenly joined me. Where from? I hadn't seen him all afternoon. He jumped up on to the ledge beside me, purring. I put out a hand, stroking him, and I then had an experience which I will always remember. I had a sense of infinite peace, as if a turbulent lake had suddenly become still. The nightmare of the past few weeks was over. Reality was ahead.

III

On Monday I spent the morning in bed. I first
stirred about ten, boiled the kettle, filled two mugs
with Darjeeling tea, and returned to bed. Two mugs
is my habit. One may become cool but I do not
mind. I have been spared getting out of bed again.

I lay there contemplating. The bedroom is so small
that the double bed takes up three quarters of the
space, and if I am sleeping on the right-hand side,
Ambrose or Cherry on the left, it is an obstacle
course to go round to the door which opens into the
sitting room.

The view from my bed is very soothing. First
there is the window where, over the years, Monty has
jumped in and out, then Lama, Oliver, Ambrose and
Cherry; and when I prop myself up against the
pillows, I look down the lane towards Monty's Leap
and the slate roof of the stables to the right where the
donkeys have their mincepies on Christmas Eve. The
lane has a scented *Tricocarpa*, a tall *Escallonia* bush, a
crab-apple tree, and willows on one side, and on the
other an untidy lace hydrangea and a May tree.
There is no human being around, and it is silent save
for the distant murmur of the sea, the croak of a

34

raven, a woodpigeon cooing, a gull calling for breakfast, a thrush and a robin singing and, on this Monday
morning, the first chiff-chaff of the spring. I lay
there, listening to its call, and remembered another
chiff-chaff, the chiff-chaff Jeannie and I heard when
first we came to Minack.

One late afternoon, it was Thursday 27 March,
we heard a chiff-chaff making its monotonous
call, the first of the year, the wonder of its
African journey transferred to Minack wood;
and it gave us the cool pleasure of confidence in
ourselves and in our surroundings. The cry
followed us: 'chiff-chaff, chiff-chaff!' . . . and
the sound of its limited note, amid trees pinking
with buds, moss brightening with growth on old
rocks, primrose a secret ecstasy unless unexpectedly discovered, pools of ragged robin and
early bluebells . . . the sound of its limited note
derided the tyranny of the automaton age and
the warped values that advance the aims of the
dodgers of truth, the cynical commentators of
the passing scene, the purveyors of mass inertia.
The dull two notes of the tiny bird trumpeted
defiance of the fake and the slick, bringing to the
shadows of the wood the expanse of its own
achievement, until the sound gently entered the
evening, and as night fell, hid among the trees.

That incident belonged to our child-like, innocent
time at Minack when we believed the possession of
enthusiasm was the secret of success; that, and a
limitless readiness for hard labouring work. The day

following our meeting with the chiff-chaff we learnt a lesson. A storm blew up, one of the most violent storms of recent years, and the gales battered our new potato crop, the crop which we depended upon for our existence, into a leafless ruin.

I lay there, remembering this, when Ambrose jumped up on to the ledge outside the window, sat there for a moment making up his mind what to do, then nosed his way through the window gap into the room and on to the bed, then up to me where he settled on my chest so that my mouth was touching his fur as he purred. It wasn't a comfortable position. I liked to think, however, that it was his way of taking special care of me. He had never been far from me during the past few weeks.

I lay there contemplating as to what Jeannie would want me to do with my life. We used to discuss, in bantering fashion, the future of the one who was left. 'Oh,' Jeannie would say to me, 'you'll marry again very quickly!' And I would laugh, answering: 'Never. I would never marry again.' And to her I would say: 'But I would want *you* to marry again, somebody rich to look after you.' And I remember the answer she always gave: 'All I want to do is to stay at Minack . . . I never, never want to leave here.'

Beyond Monty's Leap on the other side of the narrow valley I can watch from my bed the activity on Oliver land. The name Oliver land comes from the fact that we first saw Oliver in the far corner of the right of the sloping big field known in times gone by as the clover field. We saw him alertly watching a movement in the grass, then he pounced, and missed, then proceeding as cats do when they feel embarrassed, to wash himself. Oliver who was to come to Minack uninvited, and who was, in due course, to fall in love with Muffin, a cat of many colours, who lived at the farm at the top of the lane. Muffin and Oliver produced Ambrose but, as I have told in *A Cat Affair*, it was Oliver who brought Ambrose to Minack.

It was this Oliver land, twenty acres of it stretching to Carn Barges and the ancient, rough undergrowth falling down to the sea, that Jeannie and I were able to buy; and to save it from exploitation of one kind or another. It was this land for which Jeannie had a passion. So fierce was this passion that sometimes she made me believe she was instinctively convinced it was her destiny to preserve it for posterity ... preserve it, not for aggro ramblers, but for those who seek solitude, for the insects, the badgers, the foxes, the birds which travel from afar to make their nests in brambles and undergrowth; and for the wild flowers and grasses which flourish untidily in glorious, unmanaged beauty.

How uncanny it is [I wrote in *The Cherry Tree*] that, as a schoolgirl on holiday, Jeannie used to pass our land when sailing in the *Scillonian* on the way to the islands. There was her future. There was the land she was going to love so passionately.

For me, since the beginning, it has been her courage which has meant our survival. I have never seen her in despair. I can fall into depths of depression, and moan about troubles real or imaginary, but Jeannie, when I have been in one of these moods, has never given a hint of surrender. It is not a bossy kind of courage, it is a very subtle one. It has been sustained by her intense joy in small pleasures. One day in the spring she walked on her own around Oliver land; and when she returned she rushed out these words to me. 'It was so beautiful there this morning, and I only wanted to *feel* the beauty. I just wanted to *feel* the white sprays of the blackthorn, the first bluebells, the celandines and the first buttercups. I just wanted to *feel* the courting of the birds, the clap of pigeon wings, the scent of the gorse, the deep pink of the campion. I was part of all this beauty around me. I *felt* that I was, I didn't *think* it.'

I can see from my bed, occasionally, a fox gliding across the field on the way to his home in the cliff. Rabbits sometimes watch him as he passes, ears pricked, on guard. In late May and June I can observe cubs playing, tumbling, chasing each other, innocent of the dangers that lay ahead in their lives. Not just the danger of the hunt, but danger from those who shoot foxes, or poison them, selling the skins to city merchants in the fur trade.

But in the meantime they are safe if they remain on Oliver land. Everything is safe. No chance of a bulldozer tearing up the ground, heaving century ancient rocks to one side. No chance of manmade noise destroying the silence of the meadows, no chance of artificial amusement to take away the peace. A place for solitude for ever was Jeannie's dream. And as I lay in bed that Monday morning, propped up against the pillows, Ambrose purring on my chest, thinking of the times we have watched Fred and Merlin grazing slowly on the field, now soon to be Merlin and Susie, I saw Jeannie's smiling face in my mind, and her clear blue eyes shone with the courage that I knew so well. She was telling me to be cheerful, telling me that I was lucky enough to have a worthwhile motivation in my life: the shaping of her dream for Oliver land and Minack into reality.

Ambrose decided my chest was no longer a satisfactory resting place and, to my relief, he moved to the bottom of the bed, curling himself there. I stretched, propped myself again against the pillows, and went on thinking.

It is natural to feel sad for the one who is left. Sadness is there, will always be there, but there is compensation for this sadness. If you are the one who is left, for instance, you have spared the other the burden of loneliness, you have spared the other the complexity of clearing up personal affairs, you yourself are freed from the desperate worry of what might happen to the other if you had gone first. How would the other live? What about their financial survival? You have too the comfort of knowing that you were there during the closing days, and that you, instead of the other, will, in a similar time, be alone. It is for such reasons that I have long held the belief that the survivor is the favoured one. The survivor can gain inner strength by being able to prove the depth of his love. He faces all the readjustments, copes with the sorrow and the loneliness, eased by the knowledge he has spared the one he loved the agony.

I had a letter from South Africa the other day, from a stranger offering sympathy about Jeannie; and the writer told me about Dr Viktor Frankl and his book, *Man's Search for Meaning*.

Dr Frankl was a young Viennese psychiatrist at the beginning of the Hitler war, and he and his wife were taken to separate concentration camps. His wife died, so, too, did most of his family. In his book he has a chapter called 'The Meaning of Suffering', and it is from this chapter that the South African writer quoted this passage:

Whenever one is confronted with an inescapable, unavoidable situation, whenever one has to face a fate which cannot be changed . . . just then one is given a last chance to actualize the highest value, to fulfil the deepest meaning, the meaning of suffering. For what matters above all is the attitude we take toward suffering, the attitude in which we take our suffering upon ourselves.

Let me cite an example. Once an elderly general practitioner consulted me because of his severe depression. He could not overcome the loss of his wife who had died two years before and whom he loved above all else. Now how could I help him? What should I tell him? Well, I refrained from telling him anything, but instead confronted him with the question, 'What would have happened, Doctor, if you had died first, and your wife would have had to survive you?' 'Oh,' he said, 'for her it would have been terrible, how she would have suffered!' Whereupon I replied: 'You see, Doctor, such a suffering has been spared her and it is you have spared her this suffering . . .'

Of course there was no therapy in the proper sense since, first his despair was no disease and second, I could not change his fate . . . but in that moment I did succeed in changing his attitude to his unalterable fate in as much as from that time he could at least see a meaning for his suffering.

This therapeutic analysis has, however, a flaw. It helps the emotional pain but it leaves a vacuum to fill. The analysis, in its way, could apply to anyone who has lost someone very close, a child, a parent, but it doesn't fill the vacuum. One still has to face the world. One still has to force oneself to be practical. One still has to pretend to smile.

I had a certain satisfaction that, in one sphere, I had already been practical. Indeed a deeper satisfaction because what I had done was what Jeannie wanted me to do; and that was the acquisition of Susie. It had not been easy to find a donkey, but I am a member of the Donkey Breed Society, and it was through their local secretary that I heard about Susie. The local secretary had bred her, and for five years she had lived in a field close to the fire station at Truro. Then she was sold to the lady near Bodmin as I have already mentioned; and the lady was selling Susie because Susie did not seem to like the goats the lady had on her holding.

This evidence of my wish to be practical had, however, a disappointing side to it. I found I had no excitement about Susie's impending arrival on

Wednesday. Always before when a new animal was coming into my life, there was this thrill that a friend was coming, a being who would be an ally, whom, without being self-conscious about it, I could talk to with the certainty that the unburdening of my thoughts would remain for ever secret.

My father revealed to me the wonder of friendship with an animal. It was at the beginning of a school holiday when he suggested I might like to travel with him by train to Exeter where he had some business to attend to. It was a day trip. What I did in Exeter I do not remember but when, at the end of the day, we returned to Exeter station to catch the train home, my father, I remember, was looking very pleased with himself. I had no reason, at that moment, to understand why.

The train back to Cornwall set off, and after five minutes, my father, as we sat in our compartment, proposed we took a stroll along the corridor of the train. 'See what sort of people are travelling with us,' he said.

But it was not people he was intending me to be interested in. We reached the guard's van, and the guard was waiting because, of course, he had a special part in the conspiracy. My father, my quizzical father, then said to me: 'Cur,' (he always called me 'cur', I don't know why) 'Cur, go and have a look in that corner!' And in that corner I found an Old English Sheepdog puppy who, as Sir Lancelot, was to become my greatest childhood friend.

For Susie, however, I had no expectation of her becoming special. My mind was treating her in the form of a routine purchase, like a farmer who has bought cattle at market. True I had a sense of relief, but it was selfish relief. My concern about Merlin would be over, Merlin who had given me strength at times during the past few weeks ('Merlin,' I remember murmuring to him on a sombre, rainy January evening, my arms hugging his neck as he stood in the stable, 'We're losing her, Merlin, we're losing her,') would no longer be alone; and I would no longer have to lie awake, a gale blowing, rain cascading, worrying about him. Susie would take over. Susie would now have the responsibility of keeping Merlin happy.

I had finished my second mug of tea, and I must soon get up, but thoughts were tumbling through me, and I continued to lie there staring through the window towards Oliver land. There lay the key to my future, the motivation for my life. All my efforts must dwell on aiming to ensure the unspoilt permanence of Oliver land and Minack, the realization of Jeannie's dream; and as I did so I would have the knowledge that Jeannie was beside me.

I leave my diary to tell of the next few days.

25 March

I've had a down day. I've been practical but it hasn't helped. I wrote letters, paid bills in the morning and posted them at Lamorna Turn. Then I forced myself to collect the petrol can from the top greenhouse, bring it back to the Orlyt, fill up the Howard, and rotovate the vacant part of the Orlyt. I wanted to make it look clean. I don't want people to think that I'm letting things slide. Then as dusk was falling I got out the wheelbarrow and pushed it to the stables, and proceeded to fill it with the dirty straw and muck, emptying each load in the corner of the square outside. I did five loads, then spread two bales of straw on the cobbled floor. It is important for Susie to come to a clean house on her arrival tomorrow. I had also had time during the afternoon to half fix the Nature Reserve sign, but I'll get it cemented in later. I placed it at the side of the rickety farm gate amid a cluster of daffodils, Coverack Glory I think they are, and I stood back and stared at it, thinking how she had kissed it when I had taken it to her hospital room.

THE DEREK AND JEANNIE TANGYE
MINACK CHRONICLES
NATURE RESERVE
A PLACE FOR SOLITUDE

A young woman called today who has been for a long time a follower of the Minack Chronicles, bringing a bunch of iris. 'Don't remember Jeannie with sorrow,' she said, 'she would be cross if you did.'

26 March

The forecast is heavy rain around lunchtime, and Susie is due at midday. She is coming by horsebox, and the idea is to disembark her at the farm, and I'll meet her there. I've just come back from giving Merlin a breakfast of carrots, and of course I had words with him, telling him it was his last breakfast on his own, and saying that he must be polite when Susie arrives because she may be very nervous and shy at being in a strange place, especially as she has only been accustomed to small paddocks. When she finds herself in a huge field with a large strange donkey, she may take fright. It is up to you, Merlin, I said, to keep her calm and make her welcome. Merlin munched his carrots, solid Merlin, a donkey who in olden days would have been kept busy pulling a plough or a cart. Shaggy Merlin with his dark brown coat.

I broke off then to write letters, answering those who had written, and my letters were inadequate. There were hundreds of lovely letters to answer, and I hadn't the time to do them justice, and I am saying no more than 'Just to say thank you etc.,' in my handwriting. I wonder if people expect an answer, but then I think of the trouble they have taken. In my case when I am addressing envelopes, I go crazy trying to decipher the postal code of letters I receive. All take time. But it is joyous to receive such letters.

At quarter to twelve I walked up to the farm. Jack and Walter were there, and I explained that I had come to meet a donkey. And they both smiled, one of them saying that it showed I was going to stay on. 'Of course I'm staying on,' I said almost crossly, but the question was well meaning. They knew me well enough that I would never leave Minack, but the question mirrored what other people had been saying, asking me; and it made me touchy.

Twelve o'clock, and there were a few spots of rain. I stared down the lane, hoping to see the horsebox at any moment. I had by now been joined by David and Joan Wills, photographers who had taken many photographs of Minack life during the past two or three years. Their cameras were at the ready to record the arrival of Susie.

Half past twelve, and no sign of the horsebox, and the rain, from a few drops, had begun to pour. One o'clock and I had become impatient. One fifteen, and I said that we had better go back to the cottage. At one thirty, when back at the cottage, a friend on a casual visit arrived, saying he had passed a horsebox on the way, and it has almost reached the farm. Action on my part, and David, Joan and I went back up the lane. We had just reached the gate of Oliver land when we saw two figures in bright yellow oilers coming down towards us with a *tiny* donkey on a halter. She looked like a toy whose child owner had drowned it in the bath. Her legs made me think of matchsticks, and I thought how easily they could be broken. Had I made a mistake? Merlin didn't think so.

Merlin had gone berserk. Merlin on the other side of the gate was prancing like a see-saw, and making that weird noise which is the best thing he can do to emulate a proper hee-haw, and which he only emits at times of great emotion. I undid the gate, opened it ajar, then, her halter off, Susie entered the field. Bedlam!

Off raced Susie, Merlin in pursuit. Round and round they went, back legs flying, hoots from Susie which put Merlin's weird noise to shame ... all of this while the rest of us stood laughing in the rain. Then Susie came at speed towards us, put on her brakes, slid, and pulled up beside the gate, puffing. Behind her came a lumbering Merlin who looked huge in contrast to her, and he came to a stop behind her. It was Susie who demanded attention from us.

They are now in the stables, and I have just been down with a torch to see them. All is quiet. Merlin was standing in a corner. Susie was lying flat on the fresh straw. She did not move when I shone the light on her.

27 March

I woke up no longer disinterested in Susie, nor did I stay in bed contemplating. I put on a dressing gown and my Wellington boots, and went down to the stables holding a bunch of carrots. Susie was standing at the fence of the yard, Merlin framed in the doorway behind her. I held out a carrot and Susie grabbed it. Then Merlin came slowly towards me, and I held out another carrot. Merlin had no chance. Susie seized it first. Her grey coat had dried, and although she no longer resembled a drowned toy donkey, she still looked very small indeed. The black cross on her back with which all donkeys are blessed was clearly to be seen. Her pricked ears were a peculiar colour, apricot edged by black. She had an alert head and mischievous eyes, giving the impression of a donkey who would stand no nonsense. A feminist donkey, I thought. And I am wondering how Merlin will cope with her.

Later in the morning I led them both back to Oliver land, but when I reached Monty's Leap I found myself in a predicament. I had a halter in each hand, and when I reached Monty's Leap, Susie refused to cross the little stream. Merlin had already crossed and was pulling me in his zest to continue up the lane. But Susie . . . she wouldn't budge. There I was stuck in the middle of them. One pulling one way, the other pulling the other. The feminist won. The only way I was able to solve the situation was to persuade Merlin to come back across the little stream. The way was now clear for Susie to be the *first* to cross it, and this she did.

28 March

They're getting on well. They both spurned me this morning. I wanted them to come with me to the honeysuckle meadow but when I crossed the Oliver field, they ignored me. They were grazing side by side. They didn't even look up. I felt quite cross. I wanted their companionship.

29 March

I had a letter from my publishers Michael Joseph yesterday, and it was a bit unsettling. They have been taken over by Penguin, and they are now having to move from their premises in Bedford Square to purpose-built premises in Kensington. The upheaval will be enormous, just at the time *The Cherry Tree* should be receiving all the pre-publication attention. The book means so much to me because, apart from the fact that Jeannie was with me while I wrote it, she typed my muddled typescript, and drew the illustrations while she was ill. Not that she complained for a second. Indeed she said it was therapeutic to do it. It is understandable for me desperately to wish all her efforts to be a success. It is to be published in August.

30 March

I sowed mignonette in pots today, and will transplant them later in the bed on the bridge. I also sowed Busy Lizzies in pots, and planted out tulips. I bet the mice will get them. The sweet peas are growing well and I'll plant them out in the Orlyt any day now. I can never remember what the space should be between each plant, twelve inches I suppose. They are all the old-fashioned scented variety.

I was doing all this when a Dutch couple arrived. 'I hear you have lost your wife,' the man said, somewhat briskly. 'We've just come to say how sorry we are.' Then he went back to his car, and produced a box of fine cigars. 'Please accept these,' he said, handing the box to me.

People keep saying in their letters that I have such lovely memories to look back upon. It is a statement of consolation which I've used many times in the past when writing to someone in similar circumstances, believing that it was like a soothing ointment on a skin burn. Perhaps it is for many people but now it is said to me I find little comfort. I don't want to remember when there is no one to share the memories. Memories hurt. Memories bring the tears.

31 March

I must make a new Will. We had left everything to each other with the proviso that we would then devote it all to preserving Oliver land and Minack. Wills are tricky to make. Someone who is in favour at the time might be out of favour when the time comes. The new Will must be wrapped around the maintenance of the Minack Chronicle Trust which we so often talked about. It will require some hard thinking. An interim Will will be best for the moment.

1 April

The letters are so beautiful in the sense that Jeannie was loved by so many who had never even met her. For me there was always a mystery about her, and that is why life with her was so exciting. We were as one and, as I once wrote, 'We are like two islands joined together by a bridge.' I kept saying to her in these last few months: 'You're the most fascinating girl I've ever known ... and do you know why I say that? It is because the sign that a love affair is ending is when one lover says to the other: "I know everything about you" . . . but our love affair has never ended.'

Somerset Maugham wrote a paragraph about a girl which comes near to what I mean: 'You never quite got over an inner kernel of aloofness as if deep in her heart she guarded, not a secret, but a sort of privacy of soul that not a living soul would be allowed to enter.'

And this is what I wrote about Jeannie in *When the Winds Blow*, and which was read by Canon Cotter at the service:

All my years with Jeannie have been an adventure; the frivolous, glamorous times of London . . . or the first night at Minack when we slept on a mattress on the floor while the rain dripped through a hole in the roof. The companionship I have had with her has had its warmth through the unexpected. I am unable to take her for granted. She is elusive, provocative, feminine, always ready to make a sacrifice, showing faith in reality by not running away from it, always on the verge of chasing wild, imaginative Celtic dreams. No dullness with Jeannie.

2 April

I went into Penzance this morning to have a haircut, and made a fool of myself. I was walking up Causewayhead towards the hairdresser's where Bob Lang has for years trimmed my hair, when I met Michael Truscott, Michael who with John Miller has cossetted me through these past few weeks. A quick word and I was away.

But when I came out of the hairdresser's I came face to face with Michael again, and suddenly the tears – and hurriedly I left him. Same thing happened a few minutes later. I met Tony Sanders who used to be at the Savoy but now has an elegant antique shop in Penzance. I talked to him for a minute quite naturally, then again I choked.

These two incidents convinced me I must remain in the Minack citadel where I feel safe, where the ambience makes me confident. I must avoid seeing people in a foreign environment. People see me, are embarrassed, don't know what to say, then offer sympathy in the manner of asking what the weather might be like tomorrow. Difficult for them, difficult for me. Yes, stay in the Minack citadel, stock up with food and drink, set off up the winding lane only when the need to do so is essential.

3 April

I am lucky in that I've always been a loner, as Jeannie was too. I've never needed gregarious company. I have never been a group type, nor was Jeannie. No coffee mornings for Jeannie, no female gatherings, though she knew why others enjoyed them. They just happened not to be her scene. No club gatherings for me, and they too happened not to be my scene. Neither of us suited the group mentality, and we didn't care that we were unpopular in that circle. Both of us believed the thrust of life lies within oneself, and therefore one must make the effort to be true to

oneself. Yield to mass momentary hysteria, yield
to the brainwashing pushed by passing fashions
and opinions, one becomes isolated from one's
true self.

I am sitting at this moment in my usual corner
of the sofa looking up at Jeannie's painting of
Rosemodres cornfield and the farm at the top of
the lane where Jack and Alice Cockram live . . .
I have sat here in this corner of the sofa looking
up at her painting for many years, and I have
never tired of it, never failed to find inspiration
from it. What a talent has now been wasted; for
surely the test of any achievement is its lasting
ability to give sensitive pleasure.

4 April

A blaze of daffodils everywhere. Coming down
the lane the daffodils on either side resemble
troops lining the Mall on a royal occasion. Then
there are the clumps of daffodils in the hedges,
born of daffodil bulbs thrown out of meadows in
the war years when potatoes were more important than daffodils. Just by Monty's Leap there is
a spreadeagled heap of the old-fashioned *Ascania*
violets, and when the sun warms them, their
scent fills the lane. This morning I listened to a
green woodpecker knocking at a tree, hammer,
hammer, hammer, and I guessed it was making
a hole in the tree, rather than searching for the
insects that might lie in it; and I remembered
another woodpecker, another tree, one of a circle
of elms close to the cottage, where the hole was
made for the nest, where the brood was brought

to their moment to fly away . . . and the first one who did so was caught by a carrion crow.

Ambrose, named by Jeannie, loved specially by Jeannie, has been acting strangely. So much yapping, always following me about; and instead of spending the day in his customary place in the warm, wind-protecting Orlyt, he is often indoors. I have a sad sense of responsibility. I am the only human being in his life now. Every night he lies close to me. Then Cherry. She is so loving. She doesn't dare come into the bedroom. She sleeps in the spare room and, because I am one of those who yield to being conscience-stricken, I feel upset sometimes that she is there alone.

All these little matters I would have discussed with Jeannie. It is not therefore grief which is the only sorrow; silence in the cottage is the other. It is the silence which hurts.

IV

I now had to organize my life. I had joined all the others in similar circumstances. People would be watching. Can he cope on his own? Will he stay at Minack?

I was to learn that those who experience grief have to live two lives. The Queen Mother, after King George VI died, was asked how she managed to carry on with her public duties so cheerfully, and she replied: 'You should see me in my private moments.'

You have to put on a front. Nobody is more dreary than the person who carries sadness around. Hence you have to appear cheerful, so cheerful sometimes that later you feel guilty. You may think you will be criticized for not showing the conventional respect for the one you loved, son, daughter, wife, husband, parent. But if you have loved, the hurt will always be there, hidden from sight, kept in a drawer, brought out from time to time.

Grief fades, they say, but I do not want it to fade. I do not want to think of waking up one morning and going through the day without remembering Jeannie. I always want to feel she is with me. I always want to feel that her spirit pervades Minack, and that her smile is hovering in the air. Perhaps, when they say that grief fades, it is meant that grief loses its intensity. It is intense for me at the moment; and there are moments when I am mesmerized into inactivity, when I sit on the sofa looking at the armchair where she always sat, reading a book, Ambrose on her lap, and I cry out: 'Why? Why? Why?'

'She looked so young, so beautiful,' someone wrote who had visited her a few days before she died. 'She is lucky because she will always be beautiful in the minds of those who saw her.'

About the same time I had an anonymous letter enclosing this poem. I wish I knew who wrote it. An incident in the Hitler war. Grief which has remained fresh. Many, now elderly, will understand.

It seemed we were always saying goodbye,
On a crowded platform at noon,
And I thought how swiftly the minutes fly,
The train will be leaving soon.
I remember you leaned from the carriage door,
And searched my face with your eyes,
And your hand reached out to mine once more,
For this last of so many goodbyes.
It was then I heard the voice in my head,
Loudly and clearly it spoke, and said,
'The last goodbye, you'll not meet again.'
And the departing train took up the refrain,
Never again, never again,
And I wanted to shout as I watched you go,
Oh love, my love, do you know what I know?

Dry minds will call that sentimental, preferring the

manipulation of words rather than the expression of natural emotion. I have never understood why sentimentality is treated as a vice. How many times does one read, or hear, the criticism of some project as being sentimental, or being praised because it avoids being sentimental? Yet, as we see on the screens, in newspapers, in many books, the cheating qualities of mankind are acclaimed as acceptable. In excess, anything can be a sin. Yet love, in its form of sentimentality, is the least sin of all.

There was the obvious to organize. Such as meals and the caring of the cottage. I had to be the cook, but once a week Joan came and spent the day here, a Monday; and Tuesday was bliss because everything was tidied away, everything clean and polished, kitchen spotless, the carpet hoovered and the bed properly made. Joan had proved such a friend to Jeannie and me, and Jeannie loved her for her sensitive ways. I remember Jeannie saying that Joan was one of those few people she could totally trust, and that she could confide in her with the certain knowledge that what she said would never be passed on to anyone else. Not to Joan could the ancient warning be applied: 'Thy friend has a friend and thy friend's friend has a friend. Be discreet.' (A quote from Christine Foyle's beautiful anthology *So Much Wisdom*.)

Joan was a chronic animal lover, an emotional one like Jeannie, sometimes a silly one also like Jeannie. Both had ways, for instance, which I, as a one-time cat-hater, found irritating. I believed in feeding a cat in an orderly manner. I would therefore place a saucer of milk, a saucer of fish, on the carpet close to the kitchen door, using a newspaper as a tablecloth. I would then expect the cat, in the current case either Cherry or Ambrose, to come to the saucers in eager anticipation. If they didn't come, it meant they were neither hungry or thirsty, and so I left the saucers in place until they changed their minds.

The policy of Jeannie and Joan was quite different. If the saucers they put down were ignored, they would pick them up and pursue the cats, calling out: 'Fish! Milk!' One of the cats might be found lying peacefully under a bush, but a saucer would be pushed towards it ... 'Milk, Ambrose, lovely fresh milk!' would come the cry. Usually Ambrose would make a little curl of his body, as if to say: 'Please don't bother me.' But there were the occasions when he would yield to the temptation of the saucer, and there would be a cry of triumph from either Jeannie or Joan.

It has always puzzled me why those besotted by cats, any cat, want them obediently to respond to their wishes. There was a day when Beverley Nichols, the legendary cat-lover, was at Minack. Lama the little black cat was with us then, and Beverley took a special liking to her. After lunch Lama sat looking at us from the top of the back of the armchair near the fireplace. Beverley looked at her: 'I'm going to have a rest in the spare room,' said Beverley. 'I would like you to come with me.' He thereupon picked her up and carried her off: and I could see she was reluctant. Ten minutes later the door of the spare room opened, and Lama raced into the sitting room. Behind her, the great cat-lover's face peered through the gap in the doorway. 'We've had words,' he said humorously.

An example of a cat-lover's vain hope of imposing their will on a cat.

Joan is a collector of unwanted cats, not in a mass fashion but in a selective one. She looks after three or four homes during the week, and there was one home which was let to holidaymakers. The occupants told Joan they had been feeding a little grey cat with one eye, and they would have liked to take him home with them but, because of their dogs, they didn't think the cat would be happy. There was a strange feature about this cat. Every night it climbed up a tree and slept on a branch. The holidaymakers left, so what did Joan do? She toured Lamorna Valley asking whether anyone had lost a cat whose habit was to sleep in a tree, found no one who did . . . and so eventually took him home with her. He is still with her. She and Ron call him Nelson.

All this time, all this April, Joan and Ron had been specially caring. Every Monday when she came Joan would bring milk, a cake, something special for Ambrose and Cherry; and during the week, Ron would suddenly appear down the winding lane in his car, bringing fish and chips from a Newlyn fish shop, or ice cream, or a Black Forest cake bought from a shop, and when I tried to pay, they refused any payment.

One factor about these two which always amazes me is this. Ron drives a milk lorry that is based at the Unigate Depot at St Erth; and this necessitates both of them getting up at 4.30 in the morning. When, on Monday, Joan comes to clear up all that I have left during the previous week, she never at any time appears to have been up before daybreak.

When Jeannie and I went to London, Joan had the job of looking after Ambrose and Cherry, and the donkeys. Fred was still with us on the first occasion she had this responsibility; and on our return we found she had left a diary of what had happened. It was called 'The Diary of an Animal Caretaker', and the day I am quoting is a Tuesday when first she faced the responsibility of being a donkey caretaker:

Came down the lane with my usual greeting as soon as I got to the donkey's gate: 'Fred, Merlin, where are you? Fred, Merlin?' I couldn't see them anywhere; they must be all right, I'll check properly in a minute – I'll make sure Ambrose and Cherry are all right first. Yes, there's Ambrose in the Orlyt, looks at me, then curls up again. Then I see Cherry running across the path in front of the cherry tree, obviously after something. Nothing alive, just a leaf.

Mind at rest I go back to look for the donkeys. Still no sign, and I have one of my panics again. I went and collected carrots, then followed the path up on the way to the Ambrose Rock. Still could not find them and I began to imagine all sorts of things.

Then I suddenly spotted them munching away down in the lower field, so I turned back towards them, holding a carrot. As I got nearer they both came running towards me. Fred a little slower. I suddenly realised I wasn't used to donkeys, and there I was in the field with two of them. I decided to give them half a carrot each, then hang on to the other halves whilst making my

60

way back to the gate. So I started back, then found they were trotting after me. I walked faster, and they trotted faster. I wasn't really scared, just apprehensive. When I got to the gate I gave them the rest of the carrots, and they were so happy, they let me stroke them, a lovely feeling to touch them.

No fear of Joan having to go through a similar scene with Merlin and Susie. It was now the end of April, and I had come to certain conclusions. I was never going to leave Minack, even for a day, unless there was a special need to do so. I had come to realize that all I wanted to do was to be a hermit. Not in the strict sense of the word. People who came to Minack would enrich me because they would not have bothered to come, many from overseas, unless they had been on the wavelength of Jeannie and me. They have also in many instances taught us a lot, given us the mood of people in different parts of the country, different parts of the world. When we were in London, like other couples, we mixed mostly in a restricted circle of friends and acquaintances. We saw problems from a city point of view, a point of view which the Indian philosopher Rabindranath Tagore described in the following words:

The West seems to take a pride in thinking that it is subduing nature, as if we were living in a hostile world where we have to wrest everything we want from an unwilling and alien arrangement of things. This sentiment is the produce of the city-wall habit and training of mind. For in the city life, man naturally directs the concentrated light of his mental vision upon his own life and works, and this creates an artificial dissociation between himself and the Universal Nature within whose bosom he lies.

Jeannie treated these meetings with strangers very seriously. She wanted to please. She believed that if the content of books was able to relate to the feelings of the reader, making the reader want to travel a great distance, then take all the trouble of finding the place, far off the main road, no signposts, it was her job and mine to give a welcome, however inconvenient the moment might be.

I never saw her greet a stranger without a smile. So many people now remember that smile of welcome, and they have written telling me so, and how the welcome 'made their holiday'. There was no act about Jeannie's attitude. Hers was not the role of a TV star to whom people came to see for the role she played. People came to see Jeannie because the role she played was *real*, and when they met her they found a Jeannie so natural that when they left they knew they had made a friend.

Many of those who came often remembered more about the Chronicles than we did ourselves. Others would come who were far from being up to date. Thus someone, who had just read *Lama*, would ask to see Lama, and I would have to explain that she died many years before. Then there were the poignant moments. The little girl, frequently a patient in the Great Ormond Street Hospital for Sick Children needing operations, who came with her mother ...

and who threw away her calipers in excitement when she saw Fred the donkey. There was the girl who, as she lay in intensive care after being knocked down by a hit-and-run motorcyclist, said to her mother: 'I'll get better, and when I get better I'm going to Minack.' She did. She came hobbling along the cliff path, and I was to find her standing by the cherry tree with her mother. There was a look of triumph on her face.

'You see,' said her mother, 'she's talked about this moment all these months. It is this motivation which has so helped her.'

There was the girl with the broken love affair who came on a day trip from London so that she could wander around Oliver land and, as she put it, 'sort things out in solitude'. There was the young blind boy who came after listening to 'Talking Books' and who, having come down the winding lane guided by his grandparents, when he reached Monty's Leap dipped his hand in the water of the little stream, saying happily: 'I've done it!' He has been here again since then. I had a letter from him the other day. He is at a special school. He had typed the letter.

Then I remember a blind middle-aged man who arrived at the cottage with his wife and his guide dog, a Golden Retriever. Astonishingly they had walked the uneven cliff path from Porthcurno, four miles away. 'My sight,' the man was to tell me, 'suddenly disappeared within twenty-four hours.' Then he added quietly with amazing understatement, 'Very frightening for me and my family.' An example of courage that in itself enhances the pleasure of life for the rest of us.

I jump now to the summer two years after Jeannie died. On a late August Sunday afternoon, a young man in a red jersey, puffing, knocked at the porch door, and proceeded to tell me that three people were drowning, their boat having capsized, in the sea below Minack cliffs.

A week previously I had acquired a radio telephone, yielding to this break of hitherto telephonic isolation by the persuasion of an ex-Scotland Yard Crime Squad detective who possessed the franchise in Cornwall of this particular radio telephone. No outward wires were required. Just a tiny aerial, a foot high. And one special advantage was that the use of it was very expensive, even more expensive for those who might want to talk to me. Hence I had a safety net. This radio telephone would only be used in an emergency, or for other practical reasons. The cost of using it, therefore, would be the deterrent for idle gossip; and I would be spared the journey to a call box. No telegraph lines disfiguring Minack land. No name in a telephone book. I was still keeping true to the philosophy of believing we should keep isolated from instant contact with the outside world. Thus my conscience was at ease. The acceptance of this new hi-tech was justified. I did not, however, expect its justification to be proved so quickly – or that Jeannie would be the cause of its justification.

The young man in a red jersey was surprisingly calm. He was so calm that I scarcely registered what he was saying. Indeed it took several seconds for the news to sink in, further few seconds to realize that there on my Regency desk was the instrument which might save lives.

I went over to the desk, switched on the power of the instrument, then dialled 999.

'Operator,' I said as a woman's voice immediately answered, 'a boat has capsized one mile west of Lamorna, near Tater-du lighthouse, and three people are clinging to the hull.'

'I'll connect you with Falmouth Coastguard,' replied the operator quickly.

A ringing tone, on, on . . . or so it seemed.

'Operator,' I called out, my voice rising, 'Hurry, for God's sake hurry, there isn't a moment to lose, people are drowning!'

'All right, all right!' came the anguished reply of the operator, 'I'm trying to contact them. I'm trying . . .'

Then: 'Falmouth Coastguard here.'

I hurried out the information.

'Are the casualties visible?'

'From the sea, from the air, yes. But not directly from the land, too close to the cliff.'

'Information received . . . Rescue Helicopter will be on scene shortly.'

The young man now left, off to watch the rescue; and a few minutes later I heard the noise of the helicopter as it flew across Mount's Bay from the Royal Naval Air Station at Culdrose; and then I heard the roar of its engines as it hovered over the capsized boat, hauling up the three casualties. Then I went outside and watched it set off back across the Bay towards Truro and Treliske Hospital. All over in five minutes.

That seemed to be the end of the incident as far as I was concerned. An exciting Sunday afternoon, a

useful one, a dramatic inauguration of the radio telephone, and a story with which I could regale my
friends. In fact I began to do so at once. I rang up
my brother Colin. I rang up a South African friend.
I rang up, my journalistic instincts prevailing, the
local correspondent of the *Western Morning News*,
the quality newspaper of the south-west. All this was
fun; but at the time I had no idea of the significance
as to what had happened. I had no idea of the part
that Jeannie had played in it. I was to learn about
this on Monday morning.

The post had just arrived and I was looking
through it, putting temporarily aside any with a buff
envelope because I imagine such envelopes will con-
tain a circular, when there was a call outside.

'Anybody in?'

I jumped up from the sofa. 'Yes,' I said, 'I'm in!'
Remembering Jeannie's response to strangers who
have come down the long winding lane, I try to
emulate her naturalness.

'We are Carol and George Venus . . .' and Carol
Venus was holding out to me a wrapped-up cake and
a pot of jam, always so welcome. 'We have read all
the Chronicles, and we have just finished *Jeannie*.
The reading of it compelled us to come from our
home in Winchester just for the weekend . . . so that
we could see where Jeannie lived. It was yesterday
that we set out do so, yesterday afternoon. And you
know what happened to us?'

I didn't, of course, know what happened. I was
still basking in the wonderment of my radio telephone. I had no notion what part Carol and George
Venus had played . . . and Jeannie.

I was to know in detail when, after Carol Venus returned home, she wrote me this letter:

I will start at the beginning of that Sunday morning, and how we came to walk the path to Carn Barges. We first parked our car at the Merry Maidens [the stone circle, a mile or more from Minack], and walked back to the land which we thought might lead to Minack. We walked up the lane and met a farmer, Owen Prowse by name. I was very apprehensive. Owen Prowse was by the gate. We said 'Good morning' to him, and he asked us if we were on our way to see you. I, for some reason, then said we were hoping to see you, but not today as it was Sunday, and I was sure you would not want unexpected visitors on a Sunday. My husband (George) looked surprised because to all intents and purposes we *were* coming to see you. Anyway we stood chatting to Owen for about half an hour listening to some of his stories, then we walked back down the lane. All the way back George was asking me why I had changed my mind. I said I didn't know but I just didn't feel that it was right to turn up on a Sunday.

We decided to go to Lamorna Cove, and we had lunch in the little café there. After lunch we decided to go for a walk ... then I said to George, let's walk to Carn Barges, and we can take photographs on the way, and see Minack from the cliff path. Agreed on this George said he would take his binoculars. We all had a lovely walk including Jake (our dog) even though he had to be lifted over some of the rocks. We arrived at Carn Barges and decided to sit and enjoy the peace and quiet. There was no one else about. We sat on Carn Barges looking towards Minack, and I took a couple of photographs of Minack, and one of Merlin and Susie far in the distance in the field.

I then heard shouting and it appeared to be coming from the sea. I said this to George, and he said, don't be daft, there are only two boats out there in the distance, and you couldn't possibly hear anyone from there. I thought, perhaps, I was imagining things or perhaps I was hearing the lapping of the waves on the rocks below. I sat looking towards Minack, and to the far right I could see a figure. I asked George to look through the binoculars (I thought it might be you), and he said it was a lady with her hair tied back and a scarf around her neck, waving.

Then I heard the voices again, and I got quite cross and told George there was someone shouting from the sea and would he please have a good look through the binoculars. I pointed to where I thought the voices were coming from, and I could see three little black blobs in the water. The waves kept covering them and I thought perhaps it was the tip of rocks, then George spotted the upturned boat and realized three people were clinging to it!

There was no one else about except the lady . . . still in the distance.

Then we had to decide what to do . . . shall we

go for help or shall we stay to keep an eye on them, all these mixed thoughts. I then saw a fishing boat heading towards Lamorna so I took my coat off as it was a bright colour, and I waved it in the air and shouted till I was hoarse. George kept an eye on the people in the water, and on the fishing boat to see if they were coming, but I knew they were not hearing me as the wind was blowing the wrong way.

George then suggested that I went to you so you could ring for help and I said I was sure you did not have a phone . . . then two people appeared on the path, one being the man in the red jumper. We explained what was happening and he said he would run to see you and ask your help. After they had gone we spotted a jogger, and I asked him if he was going to Lamorna, and he said yes, so he, too, ran off to get help.

Then a walking couple appeared and they joined us on Carn Barges, and we shouted and shouted so that the people in the water would know they had been seen, and help was on the way. Soon after, the helicopter appeared and we knew our messengers, the man in the red jumper and the jogger, had got through with their SOS messages. But, oh dear, I had used up the film, and none left to photograph the rescue.

After the rescue I looked again for the lady who had been waving, but she had gone. George said he was sure she had been standing near your sign of the Minack Chronicle Nature Reserve where it says 'A place for solitude'.

*

One of the three in the water was a fourteen-year-old boy who could not swim, and his father was holding him up. They had been in the water at least twenty minutes, and hypothermia was setting in. Nobody had seen them till Carol and George Venus reached Carn Barges. Nobody would have ever seen them if the spirit of Jeannie had not compelled Carol and George Venus to walk to Carn Barges on that Sunday afternoon.

I am always aware of the spirit of Jeannie, and I keep remembering the verse she wrote after Penny died, and which I was to find in her desk when I was clearing up her papers.

Yet that first April, the April when I was setting out to readjust my life, I felt curiously independent of her. Emotionally I was at her mercy, and sometimes, after the post had come, and I was reading the beautiful letters of understanding, I was unable to control my tears. But on the practical side, on the need to organize my life, I was detached. I was determined not to lean on a memory. She would not have wanted me to do that.

Hence I took comfort in the fact that I had taken action in the case of Merlin, and that he now had his Susie. I was glad too that I had not ignored the Orlyt greenhouse, so that there were lettuces soon ready to be cut, and Foremost potatoes to be eaten within two or three weeks, sweet peas to pick, tomato plants firmly growing, and four Telegraph cucumber plants to produce their fruit in August. I was not so happy about the garden around the cottage. Weeds predominated, growing summer plants were absent, and there was a mental lassitude about me which stopped me doing anything about it. Perhaps this was because Jeannie always cared for the garden, and I was subconsciously hesitant to put my hands where her hands had been. As far as the rest of the land was concerned, where heavy work was required, I kept warning myself: 'Don't overdo it, do what you can but don't put yourself under stress.'

I had, however, to eat and how was I to organize this? All the years, when evening came, I could be sitting on the sofa, a drink in my hand, watching Jeannie in our galley of a kitchen preparing the evening meal, or sitting at my desk or in the hut in the wood, staring at a blank piece of paper which I was trying to fill, comfortably aware that a meal was being prepared without me having to lift a finger. It was a sacrifice on her part. She also had a book to write. She also would like to have been free. 'Why can't we get Ambrose to do the cooking?' was a perennial joke.

I was not, fortunately, ignorant of feeding myself. Indeed, before we were married, I gave Jeannie her first cooking lesson. She was staying the weekend at Cholmondley House, from where we eventually married, when I suggested to her that she cooked supper. She looked nervous. Her day life, being spent in the hotels of the Savoy Hotel company, provided her with prepared meals; and when she was at home at St Albans, her mother was the cook. Thus, when I made my suggestion, Jeannie was at a loss. I made it easy for her by proposing we had fried eggs and bacon. I showed her the frying pan, lit the gas. She thereupon put the frying pan on the gas, tossed into it a couple of broken eggs; but didn't think of putting the bacon or the fat into the frying pan. She was very upset at the result. It was our first close meeting, and she had made a fool of herself. 'Rubbish,' I said, 'forget it.' And this vulnerability on her part was to make me love her.

My form of cooking revolved around a pressure cooker, two pressure cookers in fact. Jeannie, like many others, had been scared of the pressure cooker. She did, however, admire my efforts when I played the role of a stand-in cook. She was full of praise for my soups, my onion soup in particular; and she was full of praise for my beef stew. I am not on the other hand a gourmet cook, and never will be. I could never have the patience to carry out the preparations, and I feel cheated when I watch master cooks on television, showing viewers how to serve a delectable dish. The long, tedious preparations are never shown. The various ingredients are miraculously produced, just when the final touches to the delectable dish are being made. If practical cooking was conducted in such a fashion, I would happily be a gourmet cook.

I was therefore equipped, in a simple way, to look after myself; and in reply to solicitous people who asked; 'How are you coping?' I was able to say I was coping very well. It was a white lie, of course. That April, that first April on my own, I was playing a pretending game. I did not want anyone to go away saying that I was lost without Jeannie; and when I learnt a long time later that a close connection had declared: 'Derek will disintegrate without her,' I realized what a dangerous time I had been through during those first months.

The temptation, however, when you have only

yourself to cook for, is not to cook, and have bread and cheese instead. If you live in a city there is always a supermarket to go to, or a take-away. But this situation did not exist for me, and in any case I was averse to mass-produced food. I had, however, two freezers and these provided the answer to any reluctance on my part to cook on my own. Every time I made a stew, a soup or any other dish, there was always enough surplus to go into containers for a future meal. I was therefore independent. If I planned ahead, I would only have to go up the winding lane, away from the environment of Minack, on rare occasions. Groceries and meat were delivered. The only risk I took was to fail to take my chosen dish out of the freezer in time for it to thaw.

Meanwhile I had my book *The Cherry Tree* to concern me. Publication date was scheduled for August . . . and I was remembering Jeannie in those last few months of her life. Here are my diary extracts:

21 November

Last night I thought I'd finished but Jeannie didn't like part of the last chapter, and I took her advice. Today I re-wrote the part . . . and it *is* finished! Never have I written a book under such strain, but as always my darling encouraged me and encouraged me.

What is so marvellous is that she's kept going with the typing, and I've listened to the tapping in the porch. She's up to 215 pages!

But she is having trouble with her side. Normally I would only think it was a strain because it is a finger-sized trigger point on a bone, but in the circumstances I worry and worry.

And instead of rejoicing I had finished *The Cherry Tree*, I have felt very sad this afternoon.

5 January

We spent the morning going through the chapters choosing subjects for illustration, and she is so excited about doing them. She was in sparkling form. She really seems so much better.

7 January

I had a feeling of elation during a 3 a.m. waking period in the night, that everything is going to be all right. Yet yesterday, the Christmas cards having been taken down, the decorations removed, the Christmas tree put outside, I had a feeling of apprehension. Jeannie did two delightful illustrations during the day and, as always, they are illustrations which reflect the text rather than being individual drawings. She is so shy about them and says my praise for them is an exaggeration just to make her happy. I am cross with her when she says that.

20 January

Only one more illustration to do, and she is doing it just at this moment. She is sitting at the small dining-room table by the wall where hangs her painting of Monty. She looks very intent. Typing done, illustrations done, all she can possibly do for *The Cherry Tree* has been done. I pray she won't be let down.

21 *January*

We gather the illustrations, number them according to the chapters they refer to, pack them carefully; and then I take them to Penzance station, sending them by Red Star.

Jeannie did not come with me. She stayed behind at Minack, resting.

V

Ambrose was to change his character during the summer months. All his life he had distrusted the human race, run away from anyone who had approached him, ignored the cat addicts who made seductive noises in the belief they would attract his approval. Seductive noises? Ambrose considered them insults.

I have never understood why he adopted this attitude. A case could never be made out that he had been treated cruelly when he was young, the normal explanation when an animal, cat, dog or human being, behaves in an anti-social manner. Ambrose had love from the beginning of his life. True he was born out, like a wild cat, but he was born within calling distance of Minack; and he had Oliver to love him, to take care of him as a kitten, and who was to carry him one day across Monty's Leap to a box in a garage; and where, from then on, he was loved by Jeannie.

For myself I had been intrigued by his sudden appearance, by the fact he was the double of Monty, by the magic that had brought him to Minack in such a mystical way. Yet, when I first saw him, this bracken-coloured kitten suddenly appearing out of the undergrowth a few yards away as I stood by Monty's Leap, I reacted in my usual fashion when a cat came unexpectedly into our lives.

'I'll leave you,' I said to Jeannie, 'if you feed that kitten.'

This reaction of mine, basically, has been due to my fear of the responsibilities of looking after an animal. I feel so involved in an animal that I selfishly believe it is going to interfere with my life because of my fear of the unknown. It is not only the day-to-day welfare I am concerned about but what happens if one goes away. Or if there is an accident. This outlook is stupid, but it is there.

The change in Ambrose lay in his gradual acceptance of those who came to visit Minack. Over the years there had been the regular question: 'Can I see Ambrose?' And there had been the regular answer, usually from Jeannie: 'I'll try and find him.' And off she would go scouring the possible places where he had decided to relax. Often she had to give up, no sign. Then occasionally Ambrose was discovered, and Jeannie would hasten back to the inquirer: 'I've found him . . . come softly, he's sleeping under the *Escallonia!*' Then, the camera at the ready the inquirer concerned would creep after Jeannie, and the secret hide-out would be disclosed, the camera would click and, later, a photograph of a mostly hidden Ambrose would perhaps be sent to us.

More often, however, Jeannie would return saying that she couldn't find him anywhere; and this resulted in the resigned sigh of the thwarted cat-lover: 'I expect he'll appear as soon as I've gone!'

And Ambrose usually did.

On other occasions he could be inside the cottage when there was a knock at the porch door; he might be on my lap, and the sound of the knock would send him darting into the spare room. Or he might have been roaming outside, then come in through the open window, expecting a quiet time with Jeannie and me . . . and found a stranger sitting with us. Out he would return through the window. He did not, it seemed, trust the human race.

This summer, however, when a caller arrived, he began to appear while I was talking. I might be standing on the bridge, pointing out Carn Barges to the caller, pointing out Oliver land, pointing out the pencil line of the Lizard when suddenly Ambrose would appear at my feet. The first time this occurred, I said to the caller, a little self-consciously: 'You *are* honoured!' As the summer months went by, and Ambrose repeated his gesture, the phrase became a catch phrase. I repeated it every time Ambrose suddenly appeared.

I mentioned this change in his character one day to Paul our vet who had known Ambrose over the years, and his reply was that animals sense sadness, and that Ambrose instinctively felt he had to support me. By coming to me when callers came, he was taking the place of Jeannie.

Those of logical minds will dismiss such a belief as whimsy, demanding evidence of proof, in the form of computer data as to how many cases have occurred that justify this assumption. Such people do not believe in magic. Everything has to be explained; and the explanations offered are usually negative and depressing. I prefer my father's attitude to magic. When

I was a child I asked my father why there were such colours in a sunset. He replied that I should never ask such a question. 'Just enjoy the beauty of it,' he said. He also said, 'Never question magic.'

It was a form of magic that had changed Ambrose's character, but there was a price to be paid for this support he was giving me. For instance, he would be beside me, and a visitor would say that he must be an old cat: 'You've had him a long time, haven't you?'

Such a question riled me. There was Ambrose looking magnificent, and a stranger was inferring he was coming to the end of his life.

'Good heavens no,' I would say vehemently, 'he's a young cat. Only this morning he caught a rabbit!'

I have always had a quirk which makes me avoid the measuring of time. Time, I once wrote, is a plain not a series of hills. Most of us can bring back a memory of years ago, and it is so sharp in our minds that it might have occurred an instant ago. A childhood memory, first love, or some incident which seemed trivial at the time but which suddenly re-surfaces. If one views time as a plain, there is no age barrier between the young and the experienced. They share a flow of moments of sadness, exultation, enlightenment, shock, success, failure . . . for nothing changes as the baton is passed from one generation to the next. I always sigh when I have a letter from someone who signs: 'I'm an OAP', as if it is a badge of honour.

Ambrose persuaded me that he was still young in heart by the patience he showed in catching a rabbit. He would disappear for hours, and I might worry about his absence, and have thoughts that he had been caught by a fox, or had foolishly tried to catch a stoat and had been defeated in the battle, as he once had been, when miraculously his life had been saved after the stoat had bitten his neck. These thoughts were foolish because all that concerned Ambrose was a rabbit hole, requiring on his part an endless, endless patience until the rabbit woke up in his burrow, and decided to emerge. Then Ambrose's patience was rewarded. He pounced.

Cherry's antics, however, did not concern rabbits because she found them too big for her. She performed instead those juvenile antics which enrage me. True she never has set out to catch birds (touch wood, I've never seen her with a bird), but she is a mouse catcher, and one May evening she caused me much distress.

I had been working till nine o'clock, and was about to provide myself with supper when Cherry appeared with a mouse in her mouth, a wriggling mouse, which she dropped at my feet as a gift. I bent down in an attempt to rescue it, but it disappeared underneath the sofa. I was enraged. My nerves were already on edge because of one thing and another which had occurred during the day, and the escaping mouse was enough to blow my top.

'Blast you!' I yelled at Cherry. 'Blast you! I was needing a quiet time, and now you have landed me with a mouse, and I can't have my supper, and my life has to stop while I chase it! Blast you Cherry!'

I was so cross, too cross in fact, because Cherry stared at me for a moment, frightened by my anger, unable to understand why her present was so unappreciated . . . then fled from the room through the open window of the bedroom, and away into the safety of the night. I was now left on my own to catch the mouse.

I proceeded to shut the spare-room door because I had a visitor coming on the morrow, and the mouse might run there, hide, rustle paper, and the visit would be ruined. I shut my bedroom door. We once had a pygmy mouse in our bed, brought in by Oliver, and the prospect of such an incident being repeated has always haunted me. The mouse, Cherry's mouse, therefore, was confined to the sitting room.

I thereupon set four traps. One beneath my desk. One beneath the dining-room table, two in the neighbourhood of the stove and the sofa where I believed the mouse had gone into hiding. I squished Cheddar cheese on the traps, wondering as I did so why a modern method of setting bait for a mousetrap had not been developed. An efficient, painless method. I hate on these rare occasions having to catch a mouse, but it has to be done. One mouse who was brought into the cottage by a proud cat found a nice, comfortable home in the fibre glass which retained the heat in our calor gas cooker. We tried to lure it away, but it ignored our lurings. In the end we had to engage the man who installed the cooker; and he had to take the cooker apart before the mouse budged; and it was still so intent on being free that we had to chase it as if we were riders in the Grand National. The mouse won. It eventually escaped into the garden through the front door.

Next morning the traps were intact. No squished cheese removed. No trap set off.

As I made my inspection, Cherry was watching me

from the sofa where she was sitting. There was an eerie look in her eyes. I could not define it. I can only say that I experienced an in-built feeling that she was mocking me. And, to be whimsical, I sensed she was saying to me that I was an idiot inspecting the mouse-traps.

'I caught the mouse. I did so during the night . . . *Why* did you think you needed traps?'

I do not mind having imaginary conversations with animals who are part of my life. The comfort of talking to one at a time of personal distress is so soothing because one has the ease of knowing that one's secrets will not be repeated to anyone. Yet there are those who are horrified that an animal can be a more reliable part of one's world than that of the human world.

Susie, meanwhile, was winning friends. People who had come expecting to see Merlin alone would exclaim. 'A new donkey! Oh what a pretty donkey!' Merlin, deep-thinking Merlin, was bemused. He was accustomed to receive all the attention, all the praise, and now he found himself treated as number two. He was, of course, huge in contrast to Susie. His shaggy chocolate brown coat, the bushy hair half hiding his eyes, his sturdy legs, made him resemble a burly man standing beside a slim chorus girl. Susie was so neat, so dainty.

On his birthday, 5 April, for instance, a couple came to give a present of carrots, unaware he now had a companion.

'Look Harry,' I heard the woman's voice call out as I went to meet them, 'a new donkey! Isn't she beautiful?'

Merlin and Susie were in the stable meadow, standing by the gate. Then the woman added: 'We've brought a birthday present for you, Merlin. Carrots!'

The carrots had been unwrapped. One was being offered to Merlin; and I arrived just at the time when a little grey nozzle pushed forward.

'Stop it, Susie!' I said.

But I was too late. Susie had seized the carrot, was munching it, expecting another.

'A bit pushy, isn't she?' said the woman, but in a tone that would forgive Susie anything, 'and where did she come from?'

I explained she had spent the first four years of her life in a field next to Truro fire station. The fifth year she spent near Bodmin on a smallholding whose owner had goats. The goats and Susie had not got on together.

'No wonder,' said the man, adding lugubriously, 'I shouldn't think she'll get on with Merlin either . . . being that pushy!'

She has remained pushy, but Merlin has learnt how to deal with her. Thus he will let her be in the forefront, having discovered that by staying in the background looking disconsolate there will be a sudden gush of sympathy for him.

'Oh look at poor Merlin,' someone will say . . . and 'poor Merlin' would thereupon receive the attention he had planned.

There was not, however, any doubt from the beginning that they enjoyed each other's company; and occasionally they would plot escapades together.

On the first occasion they chased a trespassing small dog out of the stable meadow, both jumping the hedge; and they chased the bewildered little dog along the coastal path towards Carn Barges, the promontory from where we first saw Minack. They were stopped by two walkers who shepherded them back to our white gate near the stable meadow; and while one walker kept them calm, the other kindly came to the cottage and informed me of the situation. They had been stopped well before reaching Carn Barges. On another occasion their escapade lasted much longer, and they went much further.

It was the morning of the London Marathon, and I was watching on television the jumbling runners running past the old buildings of London, nostalgically remembering the London I knew when front doors could be left open, when walking the streets at night was safe and a thrill. I was sitting there thinking of the price that material progress has demanded . . . when suddenly there was a knock at the door. The Marathon was just ending, and I cursed that the interruption would stop me from seeing the finish.

Mike, my good friend who lived in the farm complex, was at the door.

'Sorry to trouble you,' he said, and I replied politely that it was quite all right, believing he had come to borrow the tractor.

'You ought to know,' he went on, smiling, 'that two of the Marathon runners have lost their way.'

'Oh?' I said, puzzled.

'Yes . . . your two donkeys are down in Lamorna eating the garden of the Post Office!'

'Heavens . . . how possibly did they get there?'

It was a foolish remark because a second later I

knew how they had got there, though the measure of their achievement amazed me . . . and infuriated me.

They had jumped the same section of the stable hedge (and now it is completely blocked up) as when they chased the little dog. Yet what prompted them to do this? That I will never know. But the route they took I know. It was the route of the donkey path along which we used regularly to take Penny and Fred, then Fred and Merlin. It was a steeplechase of a path, first along the coastal path to Carn Barges, then left inland towards a copse and a stream. The stream had always been a hazard during these donkey walks, and Fred at first refused to jump it. The morning he finally decided to do so was Grand National Day. As soon as we returned to the cottage, I made an excuse to Jeannie that I had to go to Penzance; and there, at a betting shop, I backed for £5 a horse called Fearless Fred, and I gave the betting slip in an envelope to Jeannie, telling her not to open it until after the race was over. Fearless Fred came in third. Jeannie won £20.

Susie, however, had never been on this donkey walk. There had been no need for her to do so because she had the whole of Oliver land to graze in, to wander in. And so, as I reviewed the situation, I realized that Merlin, deep-thinking Merlin, must have been the instigator.

It astounds me, however, how they crossed the stream, with its awkward sloping bank angles. For Merlin it should have been difficult enough but for Susie . . . after all I had to persuade her patiently to cross the tiny flow of Monty's Leap.

Then there was the distance to go after the stream

had been crossed. They had to go along the undergrowth bounded path to the top of Lamorna Cliffs, turn left down the lane towards the Lamorna Cove Hotel, past the occasional house, past the turning to the hotel, past another turning on the left, then across the road leading to the Cove, and left again to the Post Office. Moreover they must have travelled at great speed. At eleven o'clock I had seen them grazing peacefully. At twelve o'clock Mike made his announcement that two Marathon runners had lost their way.

Mike had been telephoned by the always helpful Brian and Margaret Dodds who keep the Lamorna Post Office and shop. A few minutes after he told me, a bearded man arrived in a car to give me the same news; and he kindly offered to drive me to Lamorna. It wasn't feasible to go in my own car: I would have to walk the Marathon runners back to Minack.

We arrived at the Post Office, and there outside were Margaret and Brian and a gathering of people; and in the centre of them were Merlin and Susie, string around their necks instead of halters, looking sheepish I thought, ashamed of themselves, though no doubt glorying in the fuss that was being made of them.

'What sweet donkeys!' said one lady.

'Are they mother and daughter?' asked another.

'Spring is in their hearts!' lilted a third.

'Spring it may be,' I replied, 'but they are a damned nuisance.'

'Oh no,' tittered a fourth, 'you musn't speak cruelly about such lovely donkeys!'

I had brought their rope halters with me, and I put them on, and Brian offered to take one of the donkeys, and help me lead them back to Minack.

'In ten minutes,' I said, thanking him, 'but I've got something to do first. I need a drink!'

I thereupon led Merlin and Susie to The Wink, a hundred yards away, the ancient pub where Jeannie and I in our early days used to have such fun with the colourful Mrs Bailey, then the landlord, and our dear friend Tom, her son.

Today Bob and Di Drennan are the host and hostess, and it is a real pub, not an artificial one; the interior is filled with relics of sea-going times, beautifully polished brass mementoes, no hint of the garishness that has spoilt so many pubs; and the food they serve gives pleasure to all those who come there.

It was not, however, food that I wanted. I wanted a pint of bitter, and the mug was brought out to me and the donkeys as I stood outside beneath the winking sign of the pub. For fun, I offered Merlin the mug, and he dipped his nozzle into it; and, as this occurred, someone said beside me: 'Do you think the little grey donkey would like a lemonade?'

I then returned to the Post Office, thanking Margaret, and after that Brian and I set off back to Minack. It was to be a nostalgic journey.

We were not returning via the coastal path. Instead we went along a stretch of the main road before we turned up a path called Rocky Lane. As we went along the road a car came up behind us wanting to pass, but would Susie let it pass? I was holding the halter, and I tried to manoeuvre her to the side of the road but she refused to co-operate. Merlin, held by

Brian, was behaving sedately, but the more I tried to pull Susie to the side, the more she was determined to stay in the middle, bottom to the car. I grinned apologetically to the car driver, pointing pointlessly to Susie's behind, as if it wasn't obvious what was the cause of the hold-up. Then suddenly Susie took off, suddenly decided she had had enough . . . and there I was clinging to the rope of her halter like a man holding the rope of a balloon.

All calm again, and we were going up Rocky Lane; and nostalgia took over.

Along this lane, a path is the proper description of it, one summer's day came Jeannie and me with Penny and Fred. Jeannie wearing a slim, sea-blue trouser suit, me in grey trousers and a double-breasted dark-blue reefer jacket. Very respectable, very in tune for the task ahead. Penny and Fred were also looking respectable: Penny had a new bright red halter, Fred had a blue one. All four of us where scheduled to be on our best behaviour because we had been invited to open the Lamorna Garden Fête.

That day, timing our arrival a few minutes before that of the opening at which I was expected to make a speech, we arrived on the main road at the bottom of Rocky Lane, crossed it, and a few yards beyond faced a wooden bridge across Lamorna River which led to the field where the Fête was being held.

Penny looked at the bridge, and refused to budge.

I tugged her, onlookers pushed her, children called encouragements. Penny, black-coated Penny, born in the Connemara Hills of Ireland, was unmovable. There was only one thing we could do. We had to surrender to her, then go up the road a quarter of a

Jeannie

Jeannie with Monty

Jeannie with Oliver

Jeannie with Fred

The last Christmas

The memorial service

Ambrose at Monty's Leap

Cherry inspecting my books

Merlin and Susie photographed by a nine-year-old visitor,
James

The Nature Reserve sign

mile to a gate into a field which, after two other fields, led to that of the Lamorna Fête. Once there, of course, she behaved in the manner of Nana in *Peter Pan*. She showed such a gentle approach to children. Patiently she gave ride after ride, just as Fred gave ride after ride. Jeannie and I felt proud of them.

Now I was in Rocky Lane again, the same rocks to walk over, the same hedge and trees to pass. Nothing had changed except the passing of time.

One of grief's sudden waves hit me while I was walking up Rocky Lane. I suddenly felt her beside me, all the freshness she had, the enthusiasm, the sense, the loving, the wildness, the boldness, the qualities which made our life together a constant love affair. She was so unexpected, so critical of me sometimes, then so loving, and always courage being her flagpost.

'Shall I take Susie?' asked Brian when we reached the end of Rocky Lane, had gone up the road, then turned into the rough lane which led, a mile later, to Minack.

'Thanks,' I said, 'but I'm OK.'

I had twisted my leg and I was limping; and he had noticed it and was wanting to help. There is this quality of the permanent inhabitants of Lamorna, that they find there is much pleasure in helping. It is a natural attitude, not one actuated by theory.

We reached the gate of Oliver land, and the two Marathon runners were let loose into the field, but they were too weary to be active. They just watched us moodily, as I tied up the gate and said goodbye to Brian.

Then, alone again, I walked back to the cottage; and once again I was hit by the wave of grief.

That first summer I was on edge, and tried not to show it. I wanted to appear normal when visitors called. Many did not know what had happened, and would suddenly ask, after I had been with them for a while, 'Is Jeannie around?' And every morning the letters came, score upon score of them, and there was the constant theme: 'I never met her, though through the books I considered her as a friend.'

Sometimes people would come who had been here before, but whose names I could not remember. Jeannie and I had a way of dealing with such a situation. She would talk to them while I scurried away to look at my diary. First I would have asked them when last they had come. 'Two years ago last June' they might answer; and so it would be the diary of two years ago that I would look at, scan each day entry of June, then find the names which recalled the visitors who were talking to Jeannie. I would join them again, and I would speak the names as if I had known all along. Then there were the occasions when I was working and Jeannie would shield me, or Jeannie might be working, and I would shield her. We acted as a team; and our only object was to try to make those who came feel at ease.

On my own, however, there was always a danger of hiccups. That first summer, for instance, there was not only the problem of creating a new life for myself but there was also the stress that surrounds the publication of a new book, in this case *The Cherry Tree*. Thus, against the background of looking after myself, there was this sense of loneliness in that, for the first time, there was no Jeannie with which to face the publication; and all the time I had to display a front, like others in similar circumstances, that I was happy. I had no intention of people going away saying that I wasn't coping, and that I looked miserable.

It was this pretence that all was well which resulted in the first hiccup. As the months went by and autumn arrived, I was aware that an emotional volcano was rumbling inside me, and that at any moment it would suddenly erupt if fate decided it should do so. The events of the year were pressing on my mind. I needed kindness, tolerance and understanding. Once again I was being reminded that only those who have suffered can truly understand those who are suffering. We live in an age when every action, every thought, every emotion is rationally explained, as if we were all robots who must automatically reflect the theories drawn up by the academics who invent them. Compassion, however, is not theoretical. Compassion is bred from personal experience.

The first hiccup resulted from an 'ought'. An 'ought' is a situation in which you perform a duty which is not really necessary, when you ask someone to visit you because you feel you 'ought' to do so, and the someone accepts because he or she feels they 'ought' to accept. In my hiccup case, however, the 'ought' feeling was not as strong as I may have suggested. I truly wanted to see the two couples concerned. They were my friends. The 'ought' angle came in because I realized I had seen enough people, that I needed to relax, to start writing my book *Jeannie*. This 'ought' to see these two couples, therefore, stemmed from my wish to start my relaxation period as soon as I could. These friends would be the last visitors of the year.

Both couples arrived soon after lunchtime. One couple left at seven o'clock in the evening, the second couple left at half past nine. I was exhausted, and after we said goodbye, I sank down in the corner of the sofa and, in Churchill fashion, burst into tears. Nine months since Jeannie had died, and the emotion of those months flooded through me, all the letters I had written, all the times I had had to smile when I felt miserable ... now at last the time had come when I could be free. The last of the 'ought' had come and gone. I could now be alone. My tears were making me free.

I had sat there for half an hour when there was a knock on the door.

The second couple had returned. Their car wouldn't start. It had been raining steadily for several hours and the car, always apparently vulnerable to damp, had succumbed to the rain.

I erupted like Vesuvius.

For two minutes steam, smoke, lava, debris, cascaded around the cottage. I shouted, I behaved appallingly. Then, as suddenly as the eruption had begun, all was quiet again. I had rid myself of the pentup emotions of the past months. The poor couple had been the victims of my stress.

'Let's be practical,' I now said, 'I've got a rope, and we'll fix it to your car and to mine, and I'll drive up the lane and get your car started that way.'

The rope was fixed, and off we went. I expected the car to jerk to a start by the time we reached Monty's Leap. No luck. Up, up the lane we went.

Still no luck. We arrived at the end of the mile-long lane without a spark from the offending engine.

'Only thing we now can do,' I said, in practical fashion, 'is to leave the car here, and I will drive you home.'

The ten-mile journey was passed in normal, every-day conversation. All seemed well. It wasn't. A couple of days later a letter arrived placing me in the dock. My Vesuvius outburst was at fault. Not the car. Nonetheless I am again friends with my two friends.

There was no sign of a Vesuvius in the case of the second hiccup. It occurred a week after the publication of *Jeannie*. A delightful, elderly couple who had several times been to Minack arrived unexpectedly one afternoon with their teenage Canadian grand-daughter. I was glad to see them because Jeannie and I had found them always gentle people, and I was in the mood for gentle company. Merlin did not seem to be well, and it was soothing to have gentle people with whom I could discuss his problem. The wife helped to guide me by saying that I should leave any decision I might make to my common sense; and this I recorded in my diary that evening. I also recorded how they were 'such darlings', and that their visit had done me good.

They stayed for two hours, and I gave them tea, along with another couple who called, and I made a special fuss of the grand-daughter. I had a reason for doing this. Her mother had always kept in touch with us since she first paid a visit to Minack, an occasion when she walked the cliff path from Lamorna to Minack, three months before the girl was born; and so to celebrate the girl's 'second' visit I gave her a book, telling her not to trouble to write and thank me. All the while, however, I was worrying about Merlin, wanting to go and see him, and eventually I had to break up the tea party. As they left, as they walked off up the winding lane, I called out: 'Come again whenever you like! You are always welcome!'

Five months passed and, not that I expected to do so, I heard nothing from them. Then, at the time of the season of goodwill, when a miraculous number of Christmas cards were coming to Minack, each bearing the trouble and expense, and exuding the kindness of those who sent them, there came a letter from the couple. 'We cannot help telling you of our heavy hearts,' it said. 'Our dismissal seemed so sudden and severe after all these years.'

I was profoundly upset. Why wait five months before telling me of their extraordinary misconception? Why wait till Christmas when Minack is filled with the love and kindness of so many people, and when tears, because of the memories, are close?

I realize, of course, that I am touchy. A more detached kind of person might be unaffected by such hiccups. In my case, as it is for anyone who is experiencing an emotional upheaval, in whatever circumstances, it is understandable to be touchy and vulnerable, thus needing the special understanding of people. This particular hiccup had an effect on me, therefore, which I regret though it has now faded away. It made me suspicious of those who come here. Instead of being a person who instinctively wants to trust everyone, I found myself being on guard. I like to be open-minded and, in certain moods, disclose all sorts of feelings, say silly things, just because I like the person I am talking to, however brief may have been our acquaintance. This second hiccup made me cautious. Why drop everything I may be doing in order to give hospitality to someone who does not appreciate it?

In due course I was to realize what prompted the letter of this second hiccup. During the happy afternoon, as I was signing the grand-daughter's book and discussing when next they might come to Minack, I said as a bantering joke: 'Of course I don't want to see you again . . .' And the joke misfired. It was taken seriously!

I still do not understand why the letter came five months after that happy afternoon . . . and at Christmas time.

VI

Jeannie and I had a traditional lunch a few days after Christmas; and our guests were always Raleigh Trevelyan, Raul Balin, Michael Truscott and John Miller. Raleigh Trevelyan, the distinguished author; Raul Balin, a Spaniard who lived in London, wittily observing the artistic scene of London; John Miller, the artist; and Michael Truscott, twice winner of the prize for the top picture framer in the country and a renowned restorer of old masterpieces. Raleigh has a beautiful house off an inlet of the River Fowey. He was once an editor of my books and those of Jeannie; and he has been a stalwart, imaginative friend over the years. Jeannie and I had known John and Michael since the time we were all impoverished. I mentioned this period in my introduction to the catalogue for one of John's London exhibitions presented by the art collector David Messum.

Lunch at Sancreed House, John Miller's Cornish home five miles from Penzance, and a special occasion. Jeannie and I had been invited to a preview of his exhibition paintings; and to meet David Messum and Laura Wortley, the art historian.

'Time to leave,' I said.

Jeannie and I live at Minack near Lamorna, twenty minutes away . . . but it was years away since first we met John Miller.

We were all broke at the time. John and Michael had left London, as Jeannie and I had done, to find a new, more rewarding way of life in Cornwall.

We were struggling to survive, Jeannie and I with our flowers and early potatoes, while John, whose motivation for being in Cornwall was to paint, reluctantly had to find other ways of earning a living.

'I'm ready,' Jeannie said, and we locked the door of the cottage, and got into the car, and set off up the lane.

We met John and Michael for the first time at the Spring Flower Show in Penzance. They had rented a cottage overlooking Mount's Bay, not far from us, for six shillings a week. It was a period of time when impoverished city dwellers, genuine in their search for peace and true, not urbanized, country life, could find country cottages to live in. Jeannie and I paid twenty-five pounds a year for ours.

They moved later to a cottage at Treen, the hamlet close to the Logan Rock, and we saw them only occasionally. John, trained as an architect, now began a reputation for his skill in renovating old cottages. Friends asked him for advice, numerous friends, and John did not act like a businessman. He preferred to share his skill, not to exploit it.

'Funny,' said Jeannie, and we now had passed the farm buildings at the top of our lane and were on our way to the main road, 'that John's first real impact upon us was his design for our kitchen.' Jeannie had outlined the idea.

It was a galley-sized kitchen of pinewood drawers and cupboards, later copied by many kitchen designers.

'And all he would accept for his trouble was a calor gas refrigerator we didn't want!'

We had now reached the main road, and turned right towards Newlyn. In the distance was the spine of West Cornwall, the mystical hills of Carn Brae, Bartinney Downs and Ding Dong, farmsteads dotted here and there, and small fields enclosed by stone hedges dating back a thousand years. We went up Trevello Hill then along the winding road past Kerris on our left, and the tree-hidden one-time home of Stanhope Forbes. Now we were on the crest of Paul Hill, the sweep of Penzance below us, a glimpse of St Michael's Mount across the Bay, and the white curve of splashing sea along the front.

The turning point in John's life seemed to be a disaster at the time. He was cutting glass for a window frame when his hand slipped, and cut his wrist so severely that at first he was told he would never be able to use it normally again. I happened to call on him a few hours after he had returned from hospital, and he was in great pain.

I remember his words to me: 'I believe this was meant.'

Both he and Michael are lay Franciscan monks, and John's faith won him through. The trauma of the occasion, the long struggle to regain full use of his hand, the fear that came too, lit a spiritual fire within him. He would devote himself to what he originally came to Cornwall for. He would paint without his life being fractured by tedious interruptions. He would reflect in his paintings the subtleties of light and colour and emotion which lay deep within himself.

Jeannie and I had reached the bottom of Paul Hill and turned left up Newlyn Coombe and on to the road which leads to Land's End. Soon, after going up the hill at Buryas Bridge, we would turn right at Drift; and Sancreed House would be only a few minutes away.

'I think what I love about John's paintings,' said Jeannie, a modest painter herself, and always the illustrator of the Minack Chronicles, 'is their honesty. There is a feeling of holiness about them which I suppose is another word for truthfulness. He paints each painting as if he is a child seeing beauty for the first time.'

Sancreed House, once the vicarage, is at the edge of Sancreed Church. Jeannie and I turned into the drive.

There was never any doubt in my mind about maintaining this traditional lunch. When Jeannie was the hostess, however, I was the idle host. I would talk, pour out drinks, talk again. True I provided the main course, my special Minack casserole prepared in the pressure cooker, but it was Jeannie who made the luncheon shine. She was the organizer behind the details, the setting of the table, the laying of the White House tablecloth, the arrangement of the flowers, the attractive serving of the dishes, and the way everyone felt at ease. Some hostesses bring an awkwardness to an occasion by the fuss they make and the worry they show. Jeannie was never like that. Jeannie was so natural that a nervous guest soon became natural.

My new task as the host began, of course, with the planning; and I planned smoked salmon and creamed fresh crab as a starter, followed by the Minack casserole, followed by blackberry and apple compôte with cream, or poached Cape gooseberries with cream. As a wine I chose a Chianti after champagne before lunch.

I had, I soon found, two assistant chefs. From the beginning of my preparations Ambrose and Cherry displayed their willingness to help. The stewing steak for the casserole, for instance, was left for a moment on the porch table; and a few minutes later I saw one assistant chef, Ambrose, checking its quality.

I was aware, therefore, that the assistant chefs, keen to help me as they might be, had to be watched. There had also, for instance, been a previous traditional lunch party when the smoked salmon was left unwisely on its beautiful Meissen plate beside the kitchen stove. Ten minutes later the smoked salmon had disappeared.

I remembered that unhappy occasion as I made

my preparations; and I was determined that such an occasion should not occur again. Hence, in order to make the smoked salmon and the creamy crab perfectly safe, I placed them, the evening before, in the oven with the door closed.

About three o'clock in the morning, however, my assistant chef Ambrose who had been curled soothingly close to me all night, woke me up by pushing his cold nose into my face. For a few seconds I did not register what was happening . . . but then alarm bells rang. I sniffed something cooking. Good gracious, I said to myself, and leapt out of bed and into the kitchen. I had left the pilot light of the oven on! While I was sleeping, Ambrose curled beside me, the smoked salmon and the creamy crab were being gently cooked.

The history of anxiously prepared lunches and dinner parties is littered with such disasters . . . and also of their survival into being successes. So it was with this, my first traditional luncheon without Jeannie.

I proceeded to separate the creamy crab, now tinged with brown, from the smoked salmon. The creamy crab was clearly uneatable, but there was hope for the smoked salmon. It hadn't cooked. It was just very warm; and so I washed it in cold water, and placed it in the refrigerator. By midday it was cold; and I was sure that my guests would not possibly guess of the three-o'clock-in-the-morning drama.

Meanwhile my special casserole was being kept warm in the Hostess, also the mashed potatoes I had prepared, and the table, laid by Joan, was in place. At any moment I would be hearing the grating of tyres on the grey chippings as the first car arrived. Everything then was ready. All around the cottage, on the beams and in every corner, were the Christmas cards bringing colour to the cottage as if they were flowers; and on the top of the picture frame of Kanelba's beautiful painting of Jeannie were strands of holly, as there always has been since first we came to Minack.

Suddenly there was a strangled, choking cry at my feet. Assistant chef Ambrose was looking up at me. A discreet distance away was assistant chef Cherry.

'Good Lord,' I exclaimed, 'I'd forgotten you . . .'

The two assistant chefs were expecting a reward for their services.

I turned into the kitchen, found the plate containing the discarded crab, spooned it into two plates, handing one to Ambrose, the other to Cherry.

Within two minutes the plates were empty.

And the first car had arrived.

Four hours later there was silence again in the cottage. Another traditional lunch was a memory. All had gone well. I stood there alone after waving my guests goodbye, wishing I had someone with whom I could hold an inquest. That is what Jeannie and I would have done. We would have recalled incidents, made observations, and I might have said that I hadn't put enough salt in the casserole because I had seen Michael Truscott helping himself to more salt; and Jeannie would have said that I was inventing a complication, and that different people want different amounts of salt. Yes, all went well. Though I remembered with a sharp regret that I was so busy talking that I forgot to offer a second helping of the casserole, though perhaps they would have asked if they had wanted one. And there was another annoying, tiny incident. Just before they were about to go, I was asked by one of them for a cup of tea, and I was thrilled at the prospect of prolonging their stay. Unfortunately I couldn't find the teapot.

It was over, and dusk was falling, edged on quicker than usual by cloudy skies. I was sad but also uplifted. My friends had stimulated me. I had already started to write *Jeannie*, but now I felt imbued with a special excitement. I had much research to do, and the bulk of the research lay in the notes I have made over the years. Spasmodically all through my life I have made notes about what I am doing and thinking, and jotting down passages from authors whose thoughts are of significance to me; and by doing so I have felt I have provided a backbone to my life . . . for it is so easy to live from day to day without the discipline of self-recording; and therefore, when one wants to remember, the past is a fog.

This self-discipline has also helped me so much in writing my books. Every time I have ever conceived the idea of a book, I have begun by listing on one side of a notebook descriptions and thoughts; and on the other side a list of incidents. When I have a hundred such incidents, I sense I have the base for a book. Instead, in fact, of looking out on scenery with the door wide open, I look out, and therefore can concentrate upon, a narrow scene, as if the door is ajar. I realized, after my friends had left, that their minds had given me an impetus. In the quiet days of January, I would turn some of the pages of the notes I had made.

I needed logs, and I went outside to fill a basket. On the roof was the evening gull. Silent, wild, friendly.

So in these darkening days of January, I began to turn over the pages of my notes; and I am going to quote some of them, but in two sections. The first section reflects on London life before we came to Minack. The second section reflects various stages of our new way of life, and the exciting experiment of living it. As I read these notes, I was reliving a time shared with Jeannie.

I always found it difficult to get down to facts with my MI5 colleagues. There was so much secrecy within secrecy. My colleagues were charming and amiable, conscientious and erudite, but sometimes when I was talking to one of them a glazed expression would come over his face; and I would try to make up my mind whether he was hiding information from me or whether he felt at a disadvantage because I had shown I knew more than he did. And on occasions I felt like a small boy unwillingly let into a prefect's pow wow . . . for a sudden change of subject would take place just when I was beginning to show interest.

The KGB has always set out to discredit MI5 and MI6 because, by doing so, they scared off those who might have become potential agents of the Secret Services. Hence, after the Philby, Blunt, Burgess and Blake cases, they kept up the pressure by spreading disinformation about

Roger Hollis and Guy Liddell. The former struck me as having limited intelligence. The latter, I know, was incorruptible.

I came out of the Embankment entrance of the Savoy with Jeannie, ready to go home, when the wailing sirens sounded. We were about to get into the car but Chamberlain the Head Porter stopped us. 'The first five minutes are the most dangerous,' he said. Then we heard the flying bombs coming nearer and nearer. There were four of them, and listened to them crash, exploding in huge bangs. They were quite close; and we thought of the innocent people who had been going about their business.

The meat ration is 1/3d worth a week. Butter an ounce a week, bacon four ounces. No silk stockings available. You can buy one razor blade a week. A 12 hp car is allowed six gallons of petrol a month. Eggs are rare. There is no cheese to be had.

15 May 1943 is a date that I will always remember, the day I was told of the Holocaust by Jan Karski, one of the leaders of the Polish underground movement. He had been three times out of Poland, three times back. An incredibly brave man. I had been instructed by my chief to get his story widely circulated, and I arranged for him to meet Freddie Kuh, the head of the American Associated Press Bureau in London. I arranged lunch in one of the cubicles

at Simpson's-in-the-Strand and Freddie Kuh arrived, cynical, slick, disbelieving ... but by the end of the lunch the emotion of the story had sunk through his thick mind, and I guessed he would be thinking of it in the dark of the night with horror.

Karski, in his late twenties, slim, dark hair, a face with no smile, was ordered to rescue an elderly Polish Jew Colonel and his wife from a concentration camp. He succeeded by using false papers. One week later all the Poles in the camp were murdered.

In July 1942 Himmler declared he had a special message from the Führer that all Jews must die but they must die suffering as they were the cause of the war. Karski described to us how he was ordered to bring the news to the West, but he had to see for himself what was happening so as to be convincing. He described how there was a wooden passage leading to a railway. Thirty wagons were there. Each wagon had room for forty people. At a signal the Gestapo started shooting. The Jews in panic rushed down the wooden passage and into the wagons. When there were hundred or more in each, the Gestapo beat and shot them. 'The train shuddered with their cries,' he said. The doors were shut. But the horror did not stop there. The floors had been covered with lime. Fumes filled the wagons. The Jews died, lingeringly.

Karski then told us how the leader of the Polish underground warned him before he left Warsaw for London on his mission by saying:

'In the outside world they will never understand what it is we are trying to tell . . . you will start telling your story at 10 a.m. but at 12.30 they will look at their watches and say it is time for lunch . . . they will not understand.'

At the end of February Karski had given a special message to Sigelbaum, the leader of the Jewish Socialist party in the West. 'You *must* tell the British and the Americans that they *must* make reprisals if any Jew in Poland is to survive.' Sigelbaum said he would try. He could do no more than try.

Two days before our lunch Sigelbaum had committed suicide. He left a letter. 'I have failed,' he wrote, 'but by my death the world may be told what I was not able to tell in my life.'

I was standing on the towpath the other morning after a night of bombing, watching a pair of swans with their cygnets floating gently downstream, when a little man passed and in a cockney voice said: 'Lovely morning, sir, lovely morning.' Then he went on: 'You know, sir, whenever I wake up in the morning I say, "Thank God humanity doesn't govern the sun and the stars" . . . humanity has made a terrible mess of things . . . it's like a great big piece of indigestible meat.' He paused. 'Well, sir, I must be getting along. Lovely morning, sir, lovely morning.'

Last Sunday we had Claud and Patricia Cockburn, and Bondarenko of Tass, for lunch.

Jeannie, as has become her habit at weekends, slipped away from her St Albans' home to be my weekend hostess, and such a lovely, sophisticated one. Bondarenko is much more open-minded, more forthcoming than the usual Russian, and we discussed without effort such a wide range of political subjects. Claud and Patricia have been staying the week at the White Cross pub, but spending most of the time here at Cholmondley House while we were at work. It is interesting as to how these Communists operate. They take complete possession ... Claud has used the telephone incessantly, sent cable telegrams on it, but has made no mention of paying. It was unfortunate that Patricia lost her handbag and £15 in it on the first day, and I'm sure they think the housekeeper took it, and they may have been right. Claud is brilliant, lovable, untidy. He is one of the executive members of the Communist Party, as is Frank Pitcairn, columnist of the *Daily Worker*, and founder of the weekly, scurrilous, very well informed *The Week*. He it was who invented the phrase 'The Cliveden Set'. On one occasion when he came out to see us he arrived from the centre of London by taxi, and I mentioned that it was a strange way of sharing his money with the poor. Another time he said jokingly to Jeannie, 'When we come to power, we'll line you up against a wall and shoot you.' So full of contradictions. He is turbulent, selfish, an intellectual revolutionary, restless, a good listener, fun to be with.

*

The war drags on. The news sickens me with sadness. The vast misery and horror seems to fill the air. At night my dreams are of agonized crying men, women and children. The skies are filled with tears. The sun shines with blood.

> Went the day well?
> We died and never knew.
> But, well or ill, England
> We died for you.

The alert went at 11.40 p.m. on 16 June.

Jeannie and I were lying on a mattress in the shelter at the top of the garden. Rain was falling in buckets, and the guns barked like dogs who were not quite sure what they are barking at. At daylight the spasmodic gunfire continued until the All Clear at 9.30 a.m.

The postman called at his usual time.

'Nice day, isn't it?' he said, then added, 'lots of mysterious goings on last night.'

Our first wedding anniversary. Robert Capa, most famous war photographer of them all, was one of our guests. The alert had sounded, and he was standing at the doorway of Thames Bank Cottage, cigarette in the corner of his mouth, nonchalantly counting the bombs as they fell closer and closer, and he was calmly calling in his Hungarian accent ... one, two, three ... now us! And the anniversary party ended in debris and dust. On the sitting-room wall was the ship's clock I had bought for Jeannie that Christmas. After the roof fell in, that clock was still ticking. It is at Minack now; and still ticking.

We were with Richard Hilary one evening. His face so scarred. I will always associate him and others of his time with the glorious lines of Stephen Spender's 'Battle of Britain 1940':

> Near the snow, near the sun, in the highest
> fields
> See how these names are fêted by the
> waving grass
> And by the streamers of white cloud
> And whispers of wind in the listening sky.
> The names of those who in their lives
> fought for life,
> Who wore at their hearts the fire's centre.
> Born of the sun they travelled a short way
> towards the sun
> And left the vivid air signed with their
> honour.

I was in the Aldwych about 6.30 on Friday evening when I heard a tremendous bang. I imagined it to be a burst gas main at the top of Holborn, so near did it sound. It wasn't. It was the first V2 rocket launched on London . . . and it had landed at Chiswick about a mile from Thames Bank Cottage! The rumble that continued after the explosion was terrifying. That evening when Jeannie and I got back, Gus Foster who was landlord of The Ship next door to us greeted us by saying that we were to be his guests that evening . . . 'Better to use up the rations [of drink] before the next rocket gets us.'

*

It's all over! VE Day!

Jeannie is organizing a gigantic celebration at the Savoy. The celebrity world will be coming to it. It will all go so smoothly, and with such style. How proud I am of her. This slim, exquisite girl, so child-like yet so tough, so cool yet so feminine, will stage a production of such spontaneous joy that all present will remember forever.

The following morning we were in the American Bar with Hugh Williams (father of Simon). Hugh, or Tam, as he was known, looked wan. Suddenly he said: 'I feel as if an elderly relative spent the night in my mouth.'

There was still VJ to come, although the glory of VE day tended to make people forget the horrors of suffering that the Japanese were imposing on their enemies. Those of us, however, who were aware of the facts, rejoiced when President Truman authorized the dropping of the Bomb. His decision saved thousands and thousands of Allied lives, besides giving a warning as to what the future could hold.

The war over, and there was a strange emptiness in everybody's lives. Jeannie and I were lucky because we were happy with each other, and could live such a varied, sophisticated life. But what a jerky life we were leading. Lots of fun but where were we going? We found ourselves coming under great stress, although we were living a life which, according to the storybooks, should be free of stress. Soon it was two years since the war had ended, and we were living in a vacuum. There were so many, much less fortunate than Jeannie and me, who felt the same. During the war everyone had a worthwhile, selfless purpose, and our lives were virtually governed for us. The war had to be won. We were all together. Now we had become flotsam and jetsam, floating aimlessly along towards nowhere.

Thus it was that Jeannie and I realized that if we were to fulfil ourselves, we had to change the direction of our lives.

We arrived at midnight on Good Friday, 7 April, and here it is 24 April, and I am beginning my Minack Journal. It has been a fortnight of such discovery, unexpected emotions unfolding, delights which we had imagined but did not realize were real. On a holiday we were always so anxious to enjoy ourselves but now that we are going to live here, another dimension of pleasure has entered our lives. The sweetness of leisure, for instance. Time to do small things without fear of wasting time. Travelling the day on horseback instead of a racing car. No longer the stress that haunted us. A calmness when waking up in the morning.

Monkey (such a strange name for my mother) came on 12 April and stayed at the Lamorna Inn until 20 April. Each morning I fetched her, each evening I took her back. Praise be for the OPA 40 Land-rover. No other vehicle could have operated on such a muddy, earth-based lane as the entrance to Minack.

It was a wonderful week of happiness. She delighted in buying for us all those necessary things like scrubbing brushes, dish cloths, towels and mysterious soaps and greases which will make life, in such primitive surroundings, a little less complicated. No one gives of the spirit as she does, and her enthusiasm made every moment in her company a joy.

It has taken a long time to reach Minack, and Monkey was sad on her last day. In London we were always having long telephone conversations, a constant interchange of gossip and comments, and she is going to miss them so much. I overheard her say to herself: 'Well, it's come at last.'

For I know what it will mean to her that we are so far away . . . yet, because we are happy, she will not show that she minds.

Diary of a perfect day . . . blue sky and a soft zephyr of a breeze, breakfast of two fresh eggs which Jeannie had collected from the chicken run . . . in the wood looking for stakes for a washing line when a car arrives with potato baskets, the first car ever to reach Minack! A young man in it who had been a prisoner on the Jap railroad . . . remove barrow load of weeds to the compost heap, sprinkle it with Garotta . . . take fishing rod to rocks, sea at low tide, Jeannie bathes naked, have lunch of pâté, fish all afternoon, saw a baby seal but no fish . . . return at 7 p.m. and feed chickens, then walk up to the farm to collect milk . . . start to break in bog meadow . . . Frank Hosken, the potato dealer, calls, says we should wait till St Buryan Feast before drawing, has a look at the crop, very enthusiastic . . . have supper of fried corned beef, new potatoes and Cornish cabbage . . . shut the chickens up, play with Monty in the garden . . . Jeannie bakes three tarts and twelve tartlets and does some ironing. Go to bed at eleven.

When I called at the Agriculture Office regarding getting a grant for the well, I was asked to send a sample of the water. 'How can I?' I asked, 'if I haven't dug the well?'

Monty caught a rabbit this morning, lugged it into the cottage, and dumped it at my feet as I sat at my desk.

What a hectic time is the end of May, birds rushing around searching for food for their young, the gull treading on the garden, imperiously expecting attention, the daylight boldness of the vixen and the cubs, the heavy scent of the May trees, blackbirds chattering with a noise like castanets, lakes of buttercups, head-high cow parsley, clouds of pink campion, pools of buttercups, elderberry flowers like white plates, russet sorrel, knee-high nettles, swallows sweeping the sky, a multitude of different grasses . . . all so beautifully untamed. A jungle garden is a physical antidote to reason.

Threshing at Rosemodres on a perfect August day. The old red harvesting machine, the chaff in the breeze, the small boy William with his mock bag of corn, looking at Jeannie, surprising her with the words: 'You're a pretty bugger!' The little girl crying when told she had to go home. The cart, blue with faded red shafts, loaded with sacks of corn. The patient grey horse. The man standing on the top of the stack against the deep blue of the sky, poised, waiting for another bundle. The mouse running through stray straw. The soft breeze fanning our faces in the noon heat. The sumptuous lunchtime feast for all the workers prepared by the anxious Mrs Ellis.

Down the cliff . . . curling fronds of young bracken, a whitethroat hectically burbling, pink campion against blue elvin rock, a white spot of a yacht in the distance, a red admiral flutters by, foxgloves in odd corners, the pale shapes of the sea currents, a cormorant hurrying by, somnolent gulls on rocks, an emerald green French crabber on the way to Newlyn, curlews calling as they pass in a cloud overhead, the chuckle of a green woodpecker, a huge tanker on the horizon, Jeannie pouring out a glass of wine, fresh seaweed scents instead of car fumes, the wonderful sense of unwinding without having a timetable to unwind . . . . We are severed from fashionable distractions, we have the time to *feel* what is around us, not just to look, then take a snap for the holiday album. . . . This is a golden time. How lucky I am that Jeannie is exultantly happy.

She sits late in the evening typing her book *Meet Me at the Savoy*, with two candles flickering in bottles on the red checked tablecloth ... and, as she types, slowly, often with long intervals, our London times momentarily again fill the cottage ... and I watch her, marvelling that she is to be my companion in our great adventure during the years ahead.

Yet I find when looking through my notes that I never took the future for granted. I put down, at this time, two quotations that seemed to foresee the future, far away though it was.

This first quotation was written by the Elizabethan Sir Philip Sidney, and is called 'Epitaph'.

> His being was in her alone;
> And he not being, she was none.
> They joyed one joy, one grief they grieved;
> One love they loved, one life they lived.
> The hand was one, one was the sword,
> That did his death, her death afford.
> As all the rest, so now the stone
> That tombs the two is justly one.

This poem has a melancholy tone, but I am in sympathy with it because I am inclined to distrust those who find humour in the mechanism of life. Life is sad, not funny, as most of us will admit. Yet, the media and the fun people endlessly grind out the propaganda that we have only to laugh at the victims of laughter for our lives to be one of laughter too. Laughter, alas, is like a drug. Temporary relief only.

And there is the second quotation, from a thirteenth-century manuscript:

If thou dost harbour sorrow, let not thine arrow know it; whisper it but to thy saddle, and ride abroad with song.

VII

23 March . . . a year since Jeannie's Memorial Service
held among the daffodils in the Lama field above the
cottage; and I was now, the following day, making a
journey to London for the first time without Jeannie.
I was fussing about what to pack. Packing had always
been Jeannie's concern, and I had taken this concern
for granted. What should I take? How many shirts,
vests, pants, ties, socks, handkerchiefs, and what
about the suits? I had three. Were they suitably
pressed and clean? And shoes? One pair looked
shabby. I ought to buy a new pair. All these matter-
of-fact things had fussed me for days beforehand. I
made a list . . . take toothbrush, razor, sponge, hair-
brush, books, pipe, tobacco, ear plugs, address book,
spectacles, camera . . . I was only going away for
three days but I was behaving as if I was going away
for three months. And what about Merlin, and Ambrose and Cherry? Joan would care for them, but
that did not stop me from worrying. It is a customary
state of mind when one leaves an animal behind.
Many a holiday has been irked by the thought of the
animal who has been left at home.

I had by now drawn up the basic plan for the

Minack Chronicles Trust; and if I were run over by a bus, the object of the Trust would be in the control of the four Trustees. All four, over the years, had shown a special feeling for the magic of Minack.

There was Jane, for instance, Jane of *A Drake at the Door*, the fifteen-year-old Jane who had come barefooted to see us, asking us to give her work because she did not want to go back to school, brushing aside our hesitancy. Jane who was to win the prestigious Prince of Wales's Cup at the Penzance Commercial Flower Show for the best box of daffodils, the youngest entrant ever to do so; and who now, without conventional college training, is expert on landscape gardening.

There were also to be Associate Trustees; and my idea was that their help would be available in the event of a Philistine threat to the Minack area. They would have no executive powers but the four Trustees would contact them for their instant support if need be. I have no notion as to what they might do in such a situation. They would be the Minack SAS.

What is it, however, that I fear?

The true Cornwall is mystic. It has always attracted sensitive people who find another dimension in their lives as they wander in areas unspoilt by man, their minds refreshed by a sense of timelessness. It has been a place for dreamers, for the confused who seek to find themselves again in solitude. This is the mysticism which Cornwall has always offered; and it is now under attack.

There have, of course, always been the bucket-and-spade holidaymakers who flourish on summer beaches, but they were no threat to the dreamers.

They kept to the areas around the holiday towns, leaving the dreamers to find quiet coves, lonely stretches of cliff, free to muse, free to walk paths on their own, free to live a day in silence except for the murmur of the sea, the cries of gulls, the sigh of the wind, free to pass ancient granite barns, and old cottages, primitive in appearance. All this is now fading away. Pragmatism is taking the place of mysticism. Romance is being displaced by the ambitions of entrepreneurs and developers. The same is taking place in beautiful areas all over the world.

But I speak only of Cornwall; and it is not just remote places that are under attack. There are the towns too, where multiple stores make extravagant offers to long-established local shops, then pull them down, and erect in their place shopfronts which are equally recognisable in Wigan, Manchester or Milton Keynes; or create superstores outside the towns and, instead of profits circulating in the area, they are taken away across the Tamar to city-controlled balance sheets. Meanwhile local shops go bankrupt.

Then there are the villages where developers buy cottages, tart them up, rent them during the holiday season, and leave them empty during the winter. The community spirit of a village disappears, local shops suffer, and there is a sniff in the air that the true values of country life are being superseded by artifical values; and an imitation country life is being substituted for a real one.

There is another threat to the mysticism of Cornwall. Farmers, forced by economic circumstances to copy methods of up-country colleagues, are adopting factory methods of farming. The beauty of the countryside, the charm of ancient farm buildings, do not enter their calculations in the context of their financial survival. And that is another fear I have for the future of Cornwall . . . and of Minack.

Our long-time friends Jack Cockram and Walter Grose work the neighbouring farm. They respect the countryside. Their farm is always neat and clean, no mud around, no unsightly machinery left out in all weathers, always willing to co-operate with me, and help me specially now that I am alone. I went up the lane one morning and found Walter, eighty years old, digging out the ditch at the side of the winding lane. It was a ditch I had always kept clean myself. 'Walter,' I said, 'what are you doing? I was going to do it myself next week!'

He looked at me, leaning on his shovel, Trigger the spaniel, Whisky the collie wagging their tails beside him. Then he said gently: 'I'm doing it for *her*.' Jeannie, of course.

But Jack and Walter's time at the farm was coming to an end. They were retiring in the autumn. Who would take their place? True, I would not be personally affected unless giant tractors came to the farm, churning up the top of the winding lane. I was a quarter of a mile away, and there was the donkey field above the cottage protecting it, ensuring privacy. I would not be deeply involved, unlike Bill Trevorrow, Mike and Mary Nichols who lived within the complex of the farm buildings at the top of the lane. They would be in the centre of any change. Yet how does one reconcile the need of a farmer to earn a living, and the wish of a few for peace and quiet? Or the need of a motorway to scythe through beautiful countryside at the expense of those who had hitherto lived in tranquillity? Progress demands, it seems, sacrifice from the sensitive few.

Another price of progress is that freedom becomes choked by more and more laws. One must not flirt with a girl in the office for fear of being charged with sexual harassment. One cannot offer a lift to a woman walking home on a lonely road for fear of being accused of importunism. One mustn't smoke in public places. One has to obey race relation laws. One mustn't show affection to a child in case one is accused of potential child abuse. One cannot advertise for a man for a man's job because one will be guilty of sex discrimination. One can no longer buy true Cornish cream because milk has to be pasteurized. Towns and villages are festooned with yellow lines, stopping people from shopping. And the police, instead of concentrating their financial resources and manpower on real crime, have to deal with these surface laws, irritating the public as a consequence, often thereby losing their cooperation in serious matters as a result.

Three police officers, the other day, were employed to catch me not wearing a seatbelt at 8:30 in the morning on my way to have my hair cut. Solemn faces, notebooks in hand, they copied down details of this villain, then fined me £12 on the spot. I always wear a seatbelt. This was a unique occasion without one, and it had occurred in this fashion.

I had driven up the Minack lane to the farm and found Trigger the spaniel outside the farmhouse, wagging his tail. I stopped, undid my seatbelt in order to reach the biscuits I kept for such an occasion threw him one and another to his collie mate Whisky, then drove on ... and forgot to refasten the belt. Ironically the previous week I had given the police much help to catch a *real* villain.

As for the drink-driving laws, they have made those of us who live in the countryside social hermits. Punishing the drunken driver is an obvious necessity, but it is an affront to the freedom of the individual to treat him as a criminal because he has had a sociable drink. 'Drink and be merry!' is now a sour phrase. Cromwellian, Puritan attitudes have taken over. 'No thank you, I'm driving,' is the dreary phrase of today. If I were a dictator I would scrap the persecution of the innocent, trusting them to be sensible but free. I would instead concentrate the police manpower and resources which would then be released upon protecting the public from burglary and violence. Surely that is today's priority. Yet there would be one driving law I would be prepared to make. I would deal with slow drivers who hog the road, refusing to let cars behind them pass. Such drivers cause many accidents. They lure cars to try to pass when they shouldn't.

It seems that today's society is unaware that freedom's existence depends on the readiness to take risks. If risks are chained, freedom dies. Legislation is increasingly killing the freedom which men and women in two world wars died fighting to preserve. Freedom means people can behave foolishly, happily, imaginatively, and yet be ready to be punished if they break the fundamental rules of society. Freedom, however, demands a price. Freedom demands victims, just as those killed in the wars were victims.

Freedom cannot exist if we are perpetually cosseted by new legislation aimed at protecting us from trivial dangers.

We are therefore living in a 'take care' age. When one ends up a letter, one writes 'take care'. When one says goodbye to someone, the two words 'take care' roll off one's tongue. The whole mood of this period of time is that of 'take care'. We are deluged with advice as to what to eat, what not to eat, what exercise to take, what stereotype behaviour we should follow, the list is endless ... all aimed to maintain our existence towards a Rest Home where we can look back on our lives, having obeyed the theories but, regrettably, missed out on the sybaritic pleasures. Thus freedom is being chivvied away not just by legislation but by media influence as well. Instead of the phrase 'take care', the phrase should be 'take risks'. I first heard this phrase from a girl reader who paid a visit to Minack one day.

'Goodbye,' she said as she left. Then added: 'Take risks.'

Our idea for the Minack Chronicle Trust was a different one from the conventional conservation trusts. Such trusts are the saviour of a multitude of acres and everyone who loves the countryside should be a member of one. They are also of great educational value, and as a result it is often necessary for their organizers to treat the land under their control as a kind of public park. It is necessary for them to do so in order to fund their upkeep. Hence so many trust lands cater for the lookers rather than those who, like Hazlitt, go to the countryside to *feel*. The lookers are, of course, in the majority, and they have reason on their side. Those who *feel* are the loners. They are the eccentrics who believe, however hard the personal struggle, the quest for peace of mind lies within oneself, not by being part of the herd.

The Minack Chronicle Trust, therefore, is aimed for the loners; and because Minack is so difficult to find, no signposts, way off the main road, nature's barbed wire in the form of gorse, brambles and thorn hedges, isolating the main part from the coastal path, there is a test to pass for anyone wanting to reach the land, to reach Minack. It is a wonder for me, as for Jeannie, that so many have found their way here; and such people have come because Minack represents to them, as it always has done to Jeannie and me, a happy place. It is as if generations of happy people have lived in Minack since it was built by a crofter in the seventeenth century . . . and they are passing their happiness on.

'Something worries me,' wrote a reader after a visit. 'It's very personal of me to ask but I feel I must. What will happen to Minack and the beautiful land when you are gone? Please forgive me for probing deeply into your personal life but I feel like so many others that Minack is part of my life, just as I felt that so many of us had lost a personal friend when Jeannie died.'

The practical side of the Trust is full of mysteries. What money will be available, for instance? Supposing I live as long as Jeannie's 'uncle', Canon Martin Andrews, who was nearly 102, and who began his second book *Canon's Final Folly* on his 100th birthday? And what chance might there ever be of buying Minack itself? And there will always be the threat of a philistine entrepreneur sweeping in with an offer beyond range. When Jeannie and I conceived the Trust we, being romantics, did not go into the details; and it is for me to try to disentangle the details. I have at any rate begun to do so. I have my friends, the four Trustees. I have the Associate Trustees. But there is still so much to organize . . . I am confused. The only thing that is clear in my mind is Jeannie's determined belief that the land we owned should be preserved for *naturalness*, a place where foxes, badgers, insects, butterflies, wild plants and flowers can exist without being scientifically watched, where all nature, all sensitive minds, can share freedom in solitude.

I have a notebook in which I jot down ideas about the Trust and, on this first journey to London without Jeannie, I decided to take it with me, a way of filling the journey time. I was catching the Cornish Riviera, and I had a window seat at a small table, facing the engine. I placed the notebook on the table, a pen beside it, then looked outside as the train began to move away from Penzance station. The station is in a very beautiful setting, and the line curves around the shore of Mount's Bay, past St Michael's Mount, the sentinel of West Cornwall, and then turns inland at Long Rock. Long Rock, where Jeannie and I used to load our daffodil boxes on to the lorries which took them to Covent Garden market. Long Rock where, in our early days, we loaded our new potatoes.

I picked up the pen, fiddled with it, opened the notebook, stared at it for a few moments, had vacant thoughts, closed the notebook and looked out of the window. I was travelling my life again. There were the cottages, the tumbledown buildings, the green-houses big and small, the little fields, cows grazing, a blaze of yellow daffodils whose owner had no time to pick, a bulldozer at a building site, a wasteground of broken-up cars, all belonging to the same scene that Jeannie and I saw if we travelled to London by train.

First stop St Erth where passengers change for St Ives; and I remembered a race we had to that station at the time when we drove a Land-rover. A guest had been staying with us overlong, and we were thankful the time had come when he was going. I carried his bag to the Land-rover from the cottage, placed it in the back, started up the engine, backed, felt there was something wrong with the steering wheel and found I had a flat tyre. Panic! I changed it but slowly and clumsily and by the time it was completed I knew it was likely we would miss the train. And we did. And there was the prospect of having the unwanted guest another day. I careered into Penzance, caught sight of the train moving off, and decided to chase it to St Erth. We caught the train there. The unwanted guest was pushed aboard, and ever since St Erth station has been a happy memory.

Twenty minutes after St Erth, the railway line enters Tangye land; and by Tangye land I mean Redruth and Illogan where the Tangye family came from. Three brothers who came from a mining family and whose father was the local shopkeeper were to create at the turn of the century in Birmingham the great Tangye Engineering Works, employing two thousand people. Each, in their own way, were engineering geniuses, and their climb to fame began when Isambard Brunel sought their help to extract him from an embarrassing situation. His great steamship *The Great Eastern* had been successfully built but, having been built, it was found impossible to move the ship from the dock into the water. Then Brunel heard of a hydraulic jack patented by James Tangye, and sent an emissary to the dingy Tangye workshop in a Birmingham back street. The Tangye brothers produced the necessary jacks, and *The Great Eastern* was launched. 'We launched *The Great Eastern*,' the brothers were to say, 'and *The Great Eastern* launched us.'

William Murdock, inventor of the first railway engine (called 'Puffing Billy'), was a friend of their father; and it was outside the cottage in Redruth where the family then lived that 'Puffing Billy' had its first run.

'Murdock had built the little locomotive in his own backyard,' Joseph Tangye used to tell his sons. 'One night after his work was done down at the mines, Murdock went out with his model to the lane leading to the church to try it. He lit the lamp, the water soon boiled, and off started the engine. Murdock ran after it, but it outran him. It went past our cottage at a great rate, with Murdock running after it. Presently we heard distant shouts of terror, and found afterwards that the vicar had been scared by the engine, thinking that the hissing, spitting little demon was no other than the evil one himself.'

The vicar wasn't the only one who was scared. Later, when 'Puffing Billy' was put to work on a specially laid railway line from the mines to the village port of Portreath, the girl who was in charge of the little Tangye boys declared: 'It's a wicked thing, and you must learn to hate it, because it makes more smoke and fire to torment the poor sinners in hell.'

Here I was, a century and a half later, in the same area as where 'Puffing Billy' frightened the vicar; and I was sitting in a smoothly running InterCity train on a journey of nostalgia. A closed notebook on the table, staring out of the panoramic window as the train sped through the countryside and doing nothing but remembering.

Truro station where my mother and father used to greet me after school term's end. Truro centre where we used to shop, collect the Maascross tomato plants, four thousand of them, labelling the eventual boxes of tomatoes 'GROWN FOR FLAVOUR'. Truro where we had our first holiday together, sometimes being rowed across the Fal by Ernie, the oyster fisherman, to the pub overlooking the river at Malpas. Truro, where we stood at the bus station, waiting for a bus to take us to Newquay where I was to introduce Jeannie for the first time to my mother and father. Truro where we used to lunch at Solomito's Restaurant, Solomito one-time personal waiter to Sir George Reeves Smith, legendary chairman of the Savoy Hotel company, who turned a fish and chips shop into a restaurant acclaimed by Egon Ronay as one of the finest in Britain. Truro where as a present to myself I bought a then elaborate radio as a reward for completing *A Cat in the Window*.

I was now thinking dazily, nothing specific in my mind, just looking, as the train unfolded a kaleidoscope of pictures of the new and the old. So much that has always been; and when we passed the twisting

Fowey river, trees and undergrowth without any order on either bank, I saw the figure of myself in hip-high waterproof trousers, a Farlow rod in my hand, ready to cast a fly hopefully chosen for the momentary taste of a trout . . . but above all I remembered the pleasure I had of being alone, except for my father further up the river, who also wanted to be alone. And I used to ruminate as I stood on the river bank about the girl I would one day marry.

The railway line wends its way through the hills of Cornwall, and I have never taken for granted the marvellous viaducts of Brunel, nor ever understood how such a mammoth example of safe engineering could be achieved. Yet, I have to confess, I am always a little nervous when the train crosses the Tamar on its single line at Plymouth. All my life I have been crossing that bridge. All Jeannie's life she did too. In daytime one used to look out on a section of the fleet at anchor. The Sound is empty now. As the Cornish Riviera crossed it that morning when I was on my way to London for the first time without her, I had an irrational comfort that I was travelling on the same railway line as she had done, the last time she went to London.

I sat in my seat, gazing out of the window at the countryside flashing past, notebook unopened, vaguely observing the activities that belonged only for a second to me . . . a man mowing a pocket-size lawn, a horse grazing alone, a purpose-built factory with yellow lorries outside, lambs scurrying to their mother sheep, an incongruous sight of a red balloon above a hill in the distance, two tractors motoring a prairie field, a solitary tree in the midst of a large field making me wonder who was the romantic who had left it there, neat, spruced-up cottages, Nissans parked outside, stations that the train rushed through which were empty, forlorn . . .

My mind went back to a journey, the same journey, the same railway tracks, when Jeannie and I, just married, were returning from a blissful holiday on a farm called Treglossick near Porthallow on the Lizard peninsula. A Saturday night wartime journey, black cloth hiding the light from the windows on the travelling train. A crowded carriage. Sailors on short leave after the terror of the Northern Approaches. We were all friends in that carriage. All sleepless.

At seven in the morning we were on the platform of Paddington Station to the sound of an air-raid alarm (a false one as it turned out to be); and in a sleepy daze I carried our suitcases towards the empty taxi rank. Jeannie, meanwhile, had hurried off to the news-stand . . . and she came running back with a bundle of Sunday newspapers, calling out: 'Darling, darling . . . the most fantastic review!'

On the Monday the book I had written about the British Commonwealth, called *One King*, was to be published. And so, as Jeannie and I stood, on that chilly, foggy morning in Paddington station, we were sharing a triumph.

Now, years later, I was soon to be in Paddington station again.

The notebook on the table in front of me, still unopened.

VIII

I was in London for three days, staying at Claridge's, Jeannie's other world; and when I returned to Minack I realized I had taken a step in regaining my confidence. I realized, for instance, to what extent I had been emotionally scared of seeing again her other world, scared of being in the same streets, passing the same shops, walking through the same doors, standing in the same places, meeting the same people and recalling the multitude of incidents we had shared together. I therefore had now overcome one of the hurdles which face those who find themselves suddenly alone.

I went to London to attend the Authors of the Year Reception, given annually by Hatchards, the booksellers of world renown; and as soon as I had entered Claridge's I experienced that sense of friendship that is bred from quiet gestures, no mouthing of sad platitudes. Barry, the doorman, greeted me as I got out of the taxi by just shaking my hand, saying nothing, so too Luigi the liftman; and all during my stay was this quiet undemonstrative understanding. That first evening I went into the foyer for a drink before dining in the restaurant and, within a few moments of sitting down, the orchestra of four began to play the melody of 'Jeannie with the Light Brown Hair'. James, the head waiter, had asked them to play it specially for me. There are flowers on every table in the restaurant, and tables are well spaced, and Bruno, the *maitre d'hôtel*, gave me a table by the door where I had often sat with Jeannie, saying he thought I would like to feel she was with me; and then Luigi Previvi, an old friend of Jeannie's, and whose photograph appeared in a famous article Jeannie wrote about Claridge's for the *Gourmet Magazine* of New York, he too, before I chose from the menu, just held out his hand to me. Everyone had loved Jeannie.

My suite was on the third floor overlooking Brook Street. Our old friend Michael Bentley, manager of Claridge's, had escorted me there when I arrived. There was a beautiful bowl of flowers on a small table, and a card which said: 'Welcome to your London home' . . . and there was another bowl of flowers with a card: 'With love from all your friends at Michael Joseph'. Yes, I did feel at home. Michael Bentley sat with me for a while, talking, listening, and a sentence of his echoes in my mind: 'She looked so young, so incredibly young' . . . and I sensed there was a question he wanted to ask but was too sensitive to do so. The question: 'What went wrong?'

I arrived back at Minack in the late afternoon, and when the taxi bringing me from Penzance station drew up, I had a different kind of welcome. Merlin and Susie, for instance, were at the gate of the stable meadow, and from Susie came a soprano hoot. Merlin, hootless Merlin, just put his head on the top of the gate.

'In a moment, donkeys,' I said. 'I'll be with you in a moment.'

The taxi driver carried my two suitcases to the cottage, and as I did so, I saw Ambrose dart across the path and into the *Escallonia* bush, Escallonia Towers as we have called it because it is a sleeping place for dunnocks and blackbirds.

'Oh Ambrose,' I called out, 'don't run away!'

'Funny things cats,' said the taxi driver. 'Now if that had been a dog, the dog wouldn't have run away like that at the moment you had come home.'

I couldn't argue. A dog wouldn't have run away. It would have come to me, wagging its tail, smiling and making me feel he had much missed me. All I said to the taxi driver, a gesture in defence of a cat's contrary nature, was: 'He'll be back as soon as you've gone. Cats are shy creatures. They like to bestow love in secret. Dogs are able to display such emotions publicly. Both have the same aim.'

I let myself into the cottage. Where was Cherry, I wondered? The cottage had had a spring clean. Joan had done it to give me a surprise. Vases were filled with daffodils. A cake she had baked was in the kitchen, and beside the cake was a note describing small incidents which had occurred while I was away. 'Five callers while I was here,' said the note, 'one a French girl, very pretty! Said she'll call again.' Then another line. 'Donkeys no trouble. Couldn't find Cherry when I arrived this morning, but she came in later. Ambrose enjoyed his fish. See you Monday.'

I hauled the suitcases into the spare bedroom, changed from my suit into jeans and a jersey, and returned to the sitting room. I was not alone. Ambrose had returned; and Cherry was a discreet few feet away from him.

'Well,' I said, happy to see them, 'all three of us can now get back to normal.'

Needless to say, I had to prove it. So I went to the saucepan where Joan had left the fish, spooned enough for both plates, dumped the plates a distance from each other on the carpet beneath the bookshelf, and watched cupboard love. Or was it cupboard love? Just before he bent to his fish, Ambrose looked up at me, hesitated, and those who do not mind soppy thoughts would have interpreted his gesture as if he was saying: 'Thank you . . . I'm glad you're back.' Cherry, on the other hand, just gobbled; but when she had finished the plate, she stretched, looked at me, then came over and rubbed my leg. Yes, we were back to normal.

Dusk was falling by the time I went out to see the donkeys. I had said to them that I would be back in a moment. Half an hour had gone by, more probably, and the light was fast failing, but they were still at the gate. My hands clasped carrots as I walked towards them, and both began whinnying in pleasant anticipation. I thereupon broke the carrots in half, giving the larger half to Merlin, and I had to watch my fingers as he grabbed it. Susie had the smaller half but she munched so quickly that I was filling her mouth as if I were filling a sausage machine. Then, the carrots finished, they pushed their noses at me . . . 'more, more, more'.

I left them, walked back up the path, looked up, and there was the evening gull waiting in the dying light. He is so shy. His head weaves this way and that, as if he is scared that an enemy is following him. There is never the sound of a cry like the cries of other gulls. It is as if he is on a secret mission, a lonely secret mission. I throw up an offering, and he shows no hurry to reach it. He looks nervously around. Am I being watched? And he will wait too, until I am out of sight, before swooping down to the offering and returning to the top of the solid square seventeenth-century granite chimney. Often he is still there when night has fallen. Often, too, I forget him since, unlike the others, he does not remind me of his presence. I am then filled with remorse that he has been up there waiting while I have been indulging myself in the cottage below him, and he has been waiting, waiting for me to appear, then finally flying away, empty of attention, empty of his supper.

Ambrose curled beside me in bed that night I returned and I had the comfort of putting my hand on his soft fur, and if I pressed my hand there was a gentle purr. There were yaps too. Sometime during the night I woke up to the awareness that he was licking my face. I shifted my body, and there was a yap. I realized that, in his view, I should not have shifted. I should have stayed still, letting him continue undisturbed. I have never been able to reconcile in my mind how to deal with cat flattery at the expense of great personal discomfort. One's ego is so uplifted when a cat jumps on your lap, on your bed, that the possible consequences are ignored. Thus, when time passes, the cat is still there, cramp threatens, the ego is faced with a dilemma. Move, and the cat will jump off in bad humour. Stay, and limbs become taut, sleep becomes impossible or, if it is merely a cat on a lap, all that you were intending to do is impossible to do.

I like to pretend I have found a solution. As a one-time anti-cat person, I have still an in-built courage when dealing with a cat, even as loving as any of the cats of Minack ... Monty, Lama, Oliver, Ambrose, Cherry. My solution is to lie, or sit, in a cramped position, moving not a muscle, not a leg, not an arm, allow my neck to become unbearably stiff ... but all the while thinking of the myriad times that I have longed to discover the whereabouts of one of the cats. I think of my shouts at night. I think of the days when I have shouted their names because I wanted to show them off to some visitor. I think of the agony of my mind when, receiving no response, I have imagined that the worst has happened ... victim of a fox, run over by the postman, bitten by a stoat, kidnapped ... I think of all such distressing times as I lie cramped in a chair or in my bed. Courage then surges through me. I will take action. I will free myself of my burden. I will do it gently, with care, with minimal upheaval, but I will *do* it, and my conscience will be clear. A cat ignores my agonizing shouts. I will now ignore its comfort. Thus Ambrose on that first night of my return as he pinioned me to the bed, licking my face, yapping, was about to be a victim of my courageous intentions. I swivelled my body so that I lay on my side, and I gently pushed him away from me. What did he do? He ignored the hint. He responded by crawling back on my shoulder, pinioning me still further ... and promptly there came a trickle of purrs. Irresistible. I surrendered my courageous intentions.

I lay in bed listening to the weather forecast in the morning, Ambrose still beside me; and rain was threatened in the afternoon, and a gale. All right, I said to myself, I will get up, then go for a walk around Oliver land, go to the Ambrose Rock, wander down to the honeysuckle meadow and sit on the rickety seat. It was a blue sky, shimmering morning, idyllic sounds of birds singing, and the heads of late daffodils around the cottage were still. No wind as yet to touch them.

I had a tin of sliced peaches for breakfast, then set off down the lane, and at once experienced a small drama. Cherry trotted behind me, nonchalant, seemingly confident that she was going to be my chosen companion on the walk. Not so. Ambrose appeared, and Cherry fled. It upset me. Why could not they go on walks together? Why should they be at ease with each other indoors, but enemies outside? Ambrose was growing old. He was jealous of the young who would take his place. Just as Lama was jealous of him and Oliver.

So I was with Ambrose as I crossed Monty's Leap and went up the lane to the farm gate where there is the sign 'a place for solitude'. I climbed over Carter's stile, so named because it was built for me by a handyman called Carter who, after helping me one day, said sadly: 'I've built many walls, several stiles, created many gardens, but no one will ever know they were done by me.'

'I'll put that right,' I said, 'this stile will always be known as Carter's stile.'

I clambered over Carter's stile while Ambrose slipped under the gate, and then we went up left . . .

and Ambrose saw for the first time Jeannie's Shelter. The finishing touches had been completed while I had been away. Jeannie's Shelter, whose purpose was to house the tractor and the Condor grass cutter in one section, and a dry home for the donkeys in the other.

She always had yearned to have such a Shelter on Oliver land, and we used to have much discussion as to where it should be placed, and the discussions went on and on, and no decision was made until it was too late. Then I carried on the discussions alone with myself, and I would decide on one place, then another, then another until I become so enraged with my indecisiveness that one morning I said to myself, by midday you *must* decide, and I did; and a charming father and son whose Cornish wood buildings are built to withstand the storms were instructed to begin the work. They were very patient with me. They had erected the framework, for instance, when I decided it was too high. I had a horror that it would be a blot on the landscape. I dearly wanted the Shelter, but I didn't want it to be too obvious. There had to be a compromise; and I do now have the comfort of knowing the wood has so weathered that the shelter has become a part of its environment; and inside, the tractor is dry, and the Condor . . . and the donkeys.

Ambrose sniffed around, inspecting it, and I was half way up the side of the field, leading to the gap to blackthorn alley, before Ambrose started to follow me again. Such a slow walk but I did so welcome it. I kept pausing, looking, thinking, waiting for him to catch up with me. Blackberries were much picked by us in blackthorn alley, also by the donkeys, and by foxes who love them. Blackthorn alley has the black-berry brambles on one side and the sloes on the other. It is a narrow path, and it has to be kept cut down to keep it open, and that is part of the charm of it. It is secret. Here foxes and badgers walk, and those who seek solitude; and there is no pounding of organized walkers aiming to go from one point to another on the map, pouting complaints if the walk involved does not represent a town pavement. Here in the blackthorn alley is mystery. I can be aware of life's subtlety. I can be aware of the opposites. I can look back on the scene of Minack, on the incidents which have woven themselves into the lives of Jeannie and myself, on the calmness its environment has given us in times of distress; and on the luck that led us to a way of life that we could share together. How many, I thought, have such luck?

Yet our happiness had not been built on a placid life. We had our rows, our anxieties. We were not always virtuous in the conventional sense. We had learnt, for instance, that frustration threatens happi-ness. Satisfy frustration, therefore, and happiness endures. We lived, therefore, dangerously and did so because deep, deep down we knew that we belonged totally to each other, and that we were each other's harbour. We had learnt, too, that un-satisfied frustration can turn small incidents into major ones.

I wandered on along blackthorn alley, so full of my own thoughts that I had forgotten Ambrose; and when I turned, expecting him to be behind me, he was not there.

'Ambrose! Ambrose!' I called.

And in a few moments he emerged from the bramble undergrowth many yards behind me, and proceeded slowly towards me as if he were saying: 'I'm taking my time, taking my time!'

I strolled slowly on, reaching the badger sett which historians have told me has been there a thousand years and more. It is under an elderberry tree, the ground around it resembling a mud-packed road; and I remembered the old gamekeeper whom Jeannie and I went to see when the sett was gassed one spring before we owned Oliver land. Jeannie and I were in great distress.

'They'll be back,' said the old gamekeeper, 'nothing man can do will stop the badgers leaving the homes they have lived in for centuries.'

The persecution of badgers is endemic in sections of British society, either by baiting, or by accusing them of spreading tuberculosis among cattle. The farce of the latter accusation is summed up by the remarks of a doctor who said that if, as some declare, TB is rife among badgers, why do they multiply in numbers?

Jeannie, ferocious in her defence of the badgers, maddened by the mania of those who persecuted them and the use of gas to kill them, mischievously drafted a telegram to one of the gas advocates. 'Why evoke memories of Auschwitz?'

I passed the badger sett, Ambrose too, and I was glad he didn't pause to inspect the badger entrances. Lama did this once, and it took us hour upon hour to persuade her to come out; and my temper was such at the end that I was blasting her with words like: 'All right, stay there and get eaten!'

But Ambrose caused no trouble. He peered at a newly enlarged hole in the middle of the grassy path (and I made a mental note as he did so that I must place a stick there to warn off the donkeys or anyone else from tripping into it) then he meandered on behind me until we reached the Ambrose Rock. Jeannie believed it was a magic rock. Ambrose had given the rock its name because he had jumped up on it that first morning when Oliver land became ours. Jeannie used to go there when magic was needed in somebody's life. She would go there without telling me, and touch the rock, and say a prayer and *wish*. Two of her wishes became miraculously true. One concerned a little boy called David who was seriously ill, the other concerned a little girl called Claire; and they are both now well. Jeannie would stand by the rock, the wind blowing through her flowing dark hair, a slim figure in this untamed Cornish land, all alone, *wishing*.

I also sometimes wish. There is a spot on this granite rock where I still press my finger and wish, a secret spot. I went to that spot on the morning Jeannie went away to hospital, a foggy, wet morning. While I was there I picked a pebble from the top of the rock and brought it back to Jeannie. She took it to hospital with her. The other day I opened the purse she had with her. In it was the pebble.

We came to the rock, and I expected Ambrose to make his customary jump, followed by a crescendo of purrs as he sat there. But he refused to jump.

'Come on Ambrose,' I cajoled, 'come on, jump!'

But he didn't; and so I bent down and lifted him up. As I did so I had a wave of apprehension.

'Now purr,' I said, as if it were an order. 'I want to hear you purr.'

My tone was a reaction to my wave of apprehension. I was being silly. Why shouldn't Ambrose change his routine? Why should I be surprised? And then, just to prove my silliness, he began to purr, softly at first, louder and louder . . . and my confidence was restored.

I sat on the rock beside him for a few minutes, five, ten perhaps, time did not count because I was musing, letting my thoughts drift without any sense of order; and because there was this lack of order I was free. My mind flitted this way and that, like the way dreams dovetail without any rational connection.

For instance, I wanted to go and sit on the ramshackle seat in the honeysuckle meadow, and the mood to do so came suddenly; and I said to Ambrose that it was time to move, and as soon as I left the rock, he came too. As always he followed slowly, enjoying the sniffs, enjoying the rustles in the undergrowth which were beyond my sense of hearing. I reached the little one-foot-wide track which led off the narrow path to the Hermit's House. Jeannie and I called it the Hermit's House because it was the site, once upon a time, of a room-sized tiny building. The walls are there, three of them, the hedge bank the fourth; and one can easily imagine that it was indeed the home of a hermit who wanted to live alone within calling distance of the cliffs and the sea. We have a seat there. Sometimes Jeannie and I would sit, and say to ourselves that this was the place where we would always like to be. Then our mood changed.

The honeysuckle meadow became the place where we would always like to be.

I opened the green gate, a piece of wood on the ground beneath it marked 'Private' faded, making me realize I must re-mark it; and I entered the meadow, and went up to the seat, sat there, waited; and a few minutes later there was Ambrose coming to join me, wending his way through the grass, jumping up beside me. Now, again, my thoughts drifted without order.

Whoever is sensible, I thought, is suspicious of reason. Whoever is sensible seeks to find his guiding instinct within himself rather than being told what to do by outsiders. Whoever is sensible realizes his destiny is full of opposites. Whoever is sensible is immune from passing fashions. Whoever is sensible creates his own true values. Whoever is sensible will ignore the scientists who say don't eat that, don't do this, spoiling the enjoyment of life. Whoever is sensible is aware, instead, that his name is on the bullet, perhaps on the seat of a car or an aircraft or a train. Whoever is sensible will ignore theoretical scares in the meantime. Whoever is sensible follows the unwritten rules but retains the urge to be free in his own thoughts, in his own actions. Whoever is sensible goes through life like a metaphorical three-quarter on the rugby football field, swerving this way and that instinctively through the opposition.

Ambrose had moved from his place beside me, had put out a paw, and was now sitting on my lap. There was the sweet scent of *Ascania* violets coming from the bank behind me. A spattering of *obvallaris* daffodils; the miniature King Alfred was in the grass in front of me. Beyond, across the moorland of winter-flattened bracken and clumps of winter yellow gorse, were the sentinel rocks of Carn Barges and the sea expanse of Mount's Bay. A wren fluttered past me a foot away. From somewhere in the sky I heard the mewing of a buzzard. This was the isolation among natural beauty where Jeannie and I had said we would always like to be. I sat there, Ambrose on my lap, Jeannie beside me, thinking of the book I was writing about her.

My legs, Ambrose spreadeagled upon them, had become stiff, and I reluctantly lifted him off and put him back on the seat beside me; this did not suit him, and he was annoyed, and consequently he jumped down to the grass, and stalked off towards the green gate.

I did not immediately follow him. My thoughts were still meandering, but instead of dwelling on the past, my thoughts were dwelling on the future, the same kind of thoughts which come to everyone who has a loss.

Where am I going? What am I going to do? The first trauma is over, life is settling into a day-to-day routine, what is to be my motivation? What is to be my relationship with others? Am I just a bachelor again but without the lure of hoping to find the girl with whom to spend the rest of my life? What is to happen if I meet someone who is on the same wavelength? Someone with whom I am at ease. Am I going to feel guilty? Am I to deny myself her companionship? I sat there on the rickety bench and realized I must be prepared to lead two lives, the two lives I mentioned at the beginning of this story. One life will be the life which will surge with moments of my love for Jeannie. The second life will be facing the present, a restless present.

IX

'Cherry!' I called, 'Cherry!'

I had given Ambrose a saucer of coley for breakfast. I had another saucer for Cherry. I was standing at the corner of the cottage by the waterbutt; and I could see Cherry half-way down the lane opposite the ancient stone-capped well beneath the crab apple tree.

'Cherry!' I called again, 'if you don't hurry up, I'll give it to Ambrose.'

It was the end of April. I had heard the first cuckoo. It usually arrives on the 22nd, heralding the early morning from the rock of Carn Barges. No sign of a swallow yet. Much activity, of course, in the hedgerows, permanent residents busy feeding their young, summer visitors, newly arrived, house-hunting, checking on sites. Spasmodic daffodils still peering from banks, and in the field above the two large greenhouses there was still a white mass of the sweet-scented *Actaea*.

'Cherry!' I called impatiently.

And a strange thing happened.

The little black figure turned and fled. It jumped Monty's Leap and raced up the lane, reached the gate into Oliver land, paused, looked back for a second, then disappeared round the corner.

It wasn't Cherry. It was another black cat.

I was bewildered.

Even in my anti-cat days, as I have said, I was in favour of black cats. I felt elated if they crossed my path. Luck was now on my side in any project I was engaged in at the time. That was what I used to say to myself. As for other cats, tabby cats, mottled cats, grey cats, ginger cats, they were, as far as I was concerned, just vermin.

My attitude, of course, was to change when Jeannie's mother introduced Monty of *A Cat in the Window* in our newly married household. Monty, an autumn bracken-coloured cat, would have been vermin to me had I still been a bachelor. Instead he weaved his soul around me, and I was to love him very deeply. When he died I swore that I would never have another cat, Jeannie's passion for cats notwithstanding, unless a black cat came to the cottage door in a storm, and we could not find whence it came. A safe enough, provision, I thought, to safeguard myself from being seduced by the love of another cat.

Not so. Lama was to fulfil my proviso. She came to the cottage in a storm, and we were never to discover whence she came. And after Lama came Oliver. And after Oliver came Cherry. Black cats whose origins, and reasons for appearing at isolated Minack, we would never know.

And now, yet again, was a black cat.

It was a Monday, and Joan was soon to make her weekly arrival. I looked after myself in a moderately competent manner. I cooked my own meals, and when a visitor asked how I was coping, as if I wouldn't be coping, I was able to say that everything was fine. Someone else might be more direct, and the question would be: 'Are you eating enough?' Such kindly concern was appreciated, and yet I experienced a slight resentment that there might be any doubt about my coping. I have always been a loner; and I had learnt that the armour of the loner against moments of deep depression is inner strength. I did not have to search for company. I never went out on social visits. Minack was my world, my inner strength.

However I am one of those persons who are naturally untidy. I can spend a couple of hours tidying up the cottage, work hard at it, and yet at the end of all the effort, the cottage is untidy as ever. I can never understand why.

Joan, on the other hand, will arrive at the cottage at nine in the morning, chat for a while, then deftly move around the cottage, and within a short time puts it in order. At the end of a Monday the cottage is pristine. Clothes have been washed and dried. The cats have been fussed over . . . and, on this particular Monday, an inquisition had been carried out. The black cat, the cause.

'Joan,' I said, 'it is so extraordinary that I just can't believe it, but another black cat has come into Minack life!'

The inevitable questions followed.

'Do you know, Joan, of anyone who has a black cat?'

'Have you seen one wandering around?'

Joan was the perfect person to ask. Being a stray-cat collector, Joan is one of those people who stretches out her arms to frail animals, would never hesitate to contact the RSPCA if she thought an animal was being poorly treated. She has at her home above Lamorna valley Cindy, a one-time abandoned mongrel, whom every morning soon after daybreak (Ron her husband being an early morning milk lorry driver) she takes for a walk to the cliffs, leaving behind her cats: one-eyed Nelson, two cats Sidney and BB whose previous owners had gone to live abroad, and Sooty, a very old black cat, whom Joan and Ron were giving a home to during the ending days of her life. No better person, therefore, than Joan with whom to discuss the strange event.

But she was unable to help. She had seen no black cat around, heard of no one in the area who had lost one.

I did not see the black cat again for two days; and in the meantime I was involved, frustratingly involved, by some nitty-gritty problems. I was, for instance, becoming impatient for the arrival of the firm which I had asked to mend the Orlyt greenhouse.

In January there had been a series of snowstorms and I had been isolated for ten days. Snow drifts, hedge-high, blocked the lane. The hills of the road from Penzance halted traffic. The donkeys were stable-bound, the cats were housebound except at the beginning. In the beginning I used to carry Ambrose down to the Orlyt where the soil was snow-free, and he used to spend much of his time there curled in the bundles of hay kept for the donkeys. I didn't take

Cherry. Too risky. Ambrose would have objected. So Ambrose would be there alone in the gloom, gloom because snow covered the glass in a dense heap. He was happy there for four days. On the fifth, when I reached the door, holding him in my arms, he began to struggle; and he struggled so fiercely that I decided to take him back to the cottage. Later that day the glass roof collapsed. The accumulated snow had crushed the supports. Where Ambrose had been lying was a mass of jagged, broken glass.

I enjoyed that period of isolation. I had enough food in the freezer, enough drink to cheer me, and I had no feeling of guilt about letters I hadn't answered. And there was another bonus. I had confirmation of the friends I had. Jack Cockram struggled through the waist-high snow to see if I was all right, so too did Mike Nicholls, bringing milk and bread one day. I had gulls on the roof as company, clamouring for food, slithering down the snow-covered roof as if they were on a toboggan when I threw up a slice of bread.

Then after the snow, the thaw, and the sudden spring . . . and the assessment of damage done. The tall, treelike *Olearia* which had taken years to grow to their height, and which had proved to be a splendid windbreak, all of these silver-leafed bushes had been killed. So too the *Veronica* bushes, and the palm tree, the single palm tree, at the bottom of the cliff. All the palm trees in Cornwall were killed that January. The sudden spring came, and sleeping scents awoke, clumps of primroses appeared in hedges, in patches of grass, blue periwinkle abounded in the little garden by the porch, blue and white hyacinths perfumed the air, there were leaf buds on the Peace roses, and on the honeysuckle outside the cottage door, the scent of the sea wafted up from the cliff; Ambrose stalked down the lane towards Monty's Leap, alert to exciting noises in the grass beside the lane, Cherry bounced happily around, Merlin looked sombre, such a deep-thinking donkey, Susie looked coquettish, delighted to see a visitor; and all the while I was remembering, remembering, not the incidents that Jeannie and I had experienced, but the moments of nudging we had found to be a basic ingredient of our life together . . . 'Jeannie, I must show you this . . .' Or: 'Derek, you will understand how I feel . . .' Those were the memories which hurt. We could trust each other to understand our sudden enthusiasms, our sudden angers, our sudden depressions, our sudden triumphs or failures, knowing the emotions which might suddenly erupt would always be a secret. There where my memories lay.

I waited for the firm to come to mend the Orlyt, I waited, apprehensively, for the black cat to appear again.

'What are you calling it?' Joan had asked. 'I'm sure you'll have given it a name!'

I hadn't at the time she asked, but immediately I had replied: 'Hamlet.'

'Why Hamlet?'

'Haven't a clue. It just came out of my mouth!'

So Hamlet it was. And Hamlet was there a couple of evenings later, sitting sphinx-like in front of the escallonia in sight of the porch where I was sitting. I obeyed his demanding look. I got up, went into the kitchen, opened a tin of gourmet cat food, placed it in a saucer and took it out to him. He fled as soon as he saw me; so I put the saucer down on the ground, retreated back to the porch and waited. Not for long. Hamlet appeared again, gobbled the contents of the saucer and left.

I said I was apprehensive about him. It was the old story of not wanting a comfortable routine to be disturbed by the arrival of strangers who do not care about the comfortable routine. In human terms it happens everywhere. Isolated houses, in beautiful, peaceful areas, are suddenly surrounded by a housing estate or a motorway. Protesters are criticized for being selfish in wishing to keep their home areas immune from such an invasion. Logically such protesters are in the wrong. Progress is the arbiter of such matters. Yet morally, in the context of those who truly believe in the right of the individual to be free, these protesters are right in fighting for their freedom.

My apprehension, therefore, centred around a threat to Ambrose and Cherry. Supposing Hamlet had decided to take up residence at Minack, and was encouraged by my feeding him? What would happen to Cherry? Hamlet was a large black cat, presumably a male, and he could terrify Cherry. Ambrose, I realized, could look after himself. Not Cherry. She was too small, too gentle; and at the back of my mind was the memory of what happened to Lama when another black cat, Felix by name, decided he wanted to live with Jeannie and me.

Felix had been abandoned when a neighbouring farm had been sold. Where better, therefore, to have a new home than at Minack? He arrived one day, jumping on the window-sill of the sitting room, pressing his nose against the window where I suddenly saw him. Anxious for Lama, I went to the door and shooed him away. I felt sorry about doing it but I was glad, a few minutes later, when there was a loud hissy spitty noise outside and, on rushing out, I saw Felix racing down the path after Lama. Later that day we inveigled Felix by fresh fish so that we were able to catch him. He did not seem to mind. Nor did he show any objection when Jeannie sat in the car with Felix on her lap, while I drove him back to the abandoned farm where we knew a close neighbour would look after him. We returned to Minack, and half an hour later Felix was on the window-sill again. This procedure occurred three or four times. In the end we found someone at the coastal village of Porthcurno to give him a home. Reports reached us later that Felix had become king of the cats of Porthcurno valley.

Hamlet, handsome Hamlet, continued to appear during the coming months.

13 June

At 9 p.m. I saw Hamlet outside the porch. I opened the door and he ran to the *Escallonia*, but as soon as I put down a plate of Whiskas he came back. I watched him eat it, then opened the door again with a saucer of milk, and again he fled to the *Escallonia*, and again he came back when I shut the door. Five minutes later I looked out of the bedroom window, and surprisingly saw him and Ambrose a few yards apart eyeing each other. Then Cherry jumped through the window, seemingly very agitated.

15 June

This evening around 7.30 Hamlet was in his usual place outside the porch, and I put down a plate of supper leftovers. Strangely Cherry was in the porch window watching him, and she didn't seem to worry.

23 June

Oh dear, Hamlet seems to have taken up residence. Here for breakfast, here for supper. I took a photograph of him.

25 June

Hamlet has become a regular. I'm worrying so much about happy little Cherry. She is scared of Ambrose, so what is she feeling about Hamlet? However, no sign of him coming indoors, and he runs away as soon as I open the door.

28 June

Drama as dawn was breaking. An altercation outside in the direction of the dustbin. I jumped out of bed in time to see Hamlet hurrying past. Five minutes later, Ambrose came in through the window, jumps on the bed, looking very confident, like a boxing champion having won with a knockout. Nevertheless when I got down to the dustbin later in the morning, I found a lot of Ambrose fur on the ground.

1 July

Amazing moment this morning. I found all three, Hamlet, Ambrose and Cherry, within yards of each other, and I was lucky enough to take a photograph.

11 July

Haven't seen Hamlet for ten days. Has he gone for good? I hope so, or do I hope so?

Meanwhile I was coming towards the end of my book *Jeannie*; and I was having such a mixture of feelings. I did not want the book to end. She had been with me again. All the times, sitting here in the cottage, wrestling with the words and the incidents, I had felt the comfort of her presence. She was part of the manuscript and it seemed that she was holding my hand. Now I was coming to the end of the book, and the illusion of her presence would be ended; and I would have to wake up knowing that I was finally alone.

When the Hitler war was about to happen, I was also in a Cornish cottage, also alone. I used to sit there reading from my travel diary, writing a book called *Time Was Mine*, about my journey round the world. At that time an Old English Sheepdog was my companion. 'Roy,' I would exclaim, 'my mind is blocked, time for a walk.' And shaggy old Roy would wag his tail, and we would set off for a walk around the creeks of the River Fal.

I realize, in retrospect, that, with *Time Was Mine*, I was beginning the journey of my mind, the story of a way of life. My mother used to describe how I would amuse elderly relations (I was six or seven at the time) by strutting up and down the long verandah of our Glendorgal home near Newquay, declaiming passionate words that mirrored those of my hero, Sir Edward Marshall Hall, a famous KC who always seemed by his eloquence to obtain acquittals for those who were probably guilty.

I have no idea what prompted my hero worship, but I suspect that the seed of the idea was being sown in my mind that it was possible to influence minds, for good or evil, by reflecting the impressions of one's own life. At the time, at that six- or seven-year-old time, I was determined to be another Marshall Hall . . . until my father, a one-time barrister, said to me gently one afternoon: 'I don't think you have the kind of temperament to be a Marshall Hall. Think of trying something else!'

So now here I was again in a Cornish cottage, again alone, but with two cats as my companions instead of an Old English Sheepdog. This time I was looking through my other diaries, writing another book, looking for incidents; and I had found the entries which describe my naïve beginnings, the beginnings which were to lead me to Jeannie, a schoolgirl at the time. They made me smile. I wish I had read them to Jeannie. We would have laughed. Nevertheless without the drive behind these beginnings, we would never have met.

22 June (aged 18)

I joined Unilever on 20 October, and was placed with Mr Lightfoot in the Laundry Dept of United Exporters. There was nothing for me to do there so I was moved to GCA/UEL/MED where I still am. I am a typist and my job is to be at the beck and call of Messrs Thomas, Read and Baker. Thomas is very full of himself but has been very nice to me. Read is very fond of women as we hear from his telephone conversations, quite pleasant but not to be trusted. Baker is very pleasant but has no sense of humour.

3 July

I seem to have become a sort of professional Deb's Delight. I have had so many invitations to dances and pre-dance dinner parties. I'm sure it is because I was at Harrow. Mothers think their daughters will be sure to be safe with a Harrow boy. Last night it was a dance in Brook Street, the girl who took me there was nice, danced well, nothing out of the ordinary to say, quite pretty. Rholeu Bruce was the best girl of the lot, very pretty with a crisp way of saying things which made me laugh.

8 July

Had the most perfect dance at the Tates' last night. I went on straight to the office after a bath and an hour's rest. I felt pretty awful. Rholeu was there looking very pretty, and I had an entrancing time with her and I asked her to supper, such a pity she's leaving London at the end of the month.

15 July

Last Friday I took Rholeu to the Mayfair, my

first experience of taking a girl out to a restaurant. It was a disaster. True we danced happily to Ambrose and his Orchestra, but we had been given a table adjacent to the band, and could only hear each other if we shouted. No way for romance. Rholeu looked very pretty in a pink dress, and I wore my white tie and tails.

2 October

Had an interview with General Long today (a director of Unilever) and he said rather sadly: 'My career is just ending . . . yours is just beginning!' Just think of it! All the thrills are before me, the fun, the shocks, the shadows! Let me, therefore, not waste my chances!

6 December

I have been switched to Unilever Central Accounts, a promotion and a ten-shilling-a-week rise. What's more I have been put in charge of the Company Accounts of De Bruyn Ltd, I have to produce a monthly balance sheet, and heaven knows what's going to happen because I can't even cope with my own money problems!

10 March (aged twenty-one)

I have become a besotted admirer of Marcel Proust. Georges Cattaui who wrote a book about him in French introduced me to his work. *Swann's Way* is the first part of his novel *Remembrance of Things Past*, and it is for me a sensational beginning. I find dazzling wisdom and comfort in his writings, and answers to subconscious questions that I so often search for and fail to find. He describes feelings that I have but which I have never been able to pin down. What is more his habit of enquiring into his own thoughts encourages me to do the same. I believe that I at last have found someone to guide me in my life.

26 July

Such a red-letter day! Three months ago I started a correspondence course with the London School of Journalism . . . and today I've had my first article accepted by the *News Chronicle*! It is called 'Archers Invade England', all about the current archery craze. A start! Where will it lead me?

27 July

I was so excited by yesterday's news that I treated myself to a visit to the Ballet Russe at the Coliseum last night. How glad I am I went. It gave me entrancing pleasure, the designs were staggeringly beautiful, and beautiful to watch the human body move with such grace. And oh the music . . . the scintillating Bizet music of 'Jeux d'Enfants', and the glorious Tchaikovsky Fifth Symphony of 'Les Presages'. It was a fitting evening to mirror my happiness.

29 December

I went to the phrenologist in Ludgate Circus yesterday, a remarkable place which has been going for fifty-four years . . . no end of well-known people have had their heads bumped there! It was uncanny how the woman unfolded my faults and strengths ... she said that I had literary ability, perhaps journalism, but she said that at all costs I must not take up 'bartering or selling'. She gave me a chart of my character which I must always keep. It's so revealing.

11 February

Thank goodness for the phrenologist! Yesterday I was interviewed by two Unilever directors, and today I was informed that I had been chosen to be a travelling salesman for the soap manufacturers J. Crosfield and Sons; and that my base would be at Warrington in Lancashire for two years or so, and that I had to leave by the 8.30 train on Monday! The salary was £175 plus hotel expenses. Think of all those among the two million unemployed who would have jumped at the chance. But I have refused! I have no intention of being a soap salesman for the rest of my life ... but it was the lady phrenologist who gave me the confidence to refuse!

18 March (aged twenty-two)

I've left Unilever! There have been all sorts of goings on. One director got me into Lintas, their advertising agency, and after three weeks its manager said I was doing very well. Then the staff manager said the director had no authority to put me into Lintas, and all hell was let loose. In the end I bounced out, fed up with them all. And so I am free! Free to do what? Oh what a blessed moment this is. I now can follow my own road instead of big business.

2 *April*

Another job offered me, and again I've refused! Vick Chemicals chose me out of dozens of applicants to be a salesman for their products, but again I remembered the advice of the lady phrenologist. Something deep down tells me I'm right. Of course I am looking for a job, a temporary job; and why in this uncertain world look for anything else? The trouble is that I'm lazy, and I lack confidence, and I hate myself when I'm in a party. Always talking too vigorously.

19 *April*

Letter from Mother today which should be framed in a golden frame and preserved in the British Museum as the perfect letter from a mother to her wandering son; and she enclosed £6 for me to take a short story course. And my lovable, easy-to-be-with father has said he'll give me £2 a week.

20 *June*

No job in sight. But being a Deb's Delight is very useful. I return in the early morning to Joubert Studios (off the King's Road, Chelsea) with the pockets of my tails full of delicacies from the buffet table of the dance I'd been to; and that keeps me in food for the day. Last night the food came from the Lord Camrose dance, a very elegant occasion.

10 July

I now have no wish to take up a career with a future to it. All I want to do is to have a job that for the moment is congenial. It is too big a risk to slave away one's youth in order to gratify the faint hope of making a lot of money in twenty years' time. The world is in such a turmoil that there can be no advantage in playing safe. Sometime there will be another war; and so I say, live every moment of my life, get every bit of pleasure out of it, and let the future take care of itself.

11 July

Read yesterday's entry just now, then thought how I could only talk like that because I have a mother and father who believe in me. Daddy wrote the other day: 'You haven't got the job you wanted yet, but you know where you are going. That's the important thing. Keep your pecker up. The opportunity will come.'

I feel guilty about Mother (or Monkey as we incongruously call her) for during this period of my unemployment she has been supporting me in a racing betting scheme which I had persuaded her into believing was infallible. It isn't infallible. Not up to now.

15 July

I sense something is happening. I've been taking out a girl who has a close friend who knows Max Aitken, son of Beaverbrook of the *Daily Express*, and she is going to ask her friend to ask Max Aitken to give me an interview. And the interview occurred today, and I really felt it was a happy interview!

22 *August*

It's happened! I've been given a month's trial on the *Daily Express* in Manchester, and all the result of the girl who had a friend who knew Max Aitken! I'm a bit scared. At the moment I'm at Seaview on the Isle of Wight, and having a lovely superficial time with the Baxters. James Mason is staying here too. He is very quiet and possesses a peculiar, languorous charm. One sees in his face a great deal of his character . . . loyal, a sense of humour, and any amount of intelligence.

I keep talking to myself about Manchester. I must go with any amount of self-confidence and bluff. It is a curious feeling but deep inside me I am feeling I'm going to make a success of it.

2 *September*

My first night in Manchester! I arrived in mid-afternoon and I trundled round looking for rooms until finally I came to No. 18 Ackers Street where I'm paying £1 a week. It is very forlorn but I'll manage.

And tomorrow I start my new career. Curiously I don't feel now all that apprehensive, but perhaps when tomorrow I have to face the facts I'll be scared. Oh heavens! What a chance I have before me! Am I equal to it? If I don't make it, I don't dare think what will happen to me.

Four years later Jeannie, as she walked to her office where she was a secretary, observed the face of Derek Tangye fronting the buses as they travelled London streets, accompanied by the caption: 'READ DEREK TANGYE'.

Who is he? she murmured to herself. Why should he have so much publicity?

Five years later we married.

X

I am sad today.

I open a drawer and there is a purse, untouched since last she used it. Belts for her little waist are there too, green belts, red belts, yellow belts; and there is a black satin evening bag edged with gold ribbon, reminding me of our last dinner party at Claridge's. All day I had been leading my other life, my forgetting life, pursuing my work, laughing, joking, my mind oblivious of what had happened . . . and now these reminders, and the sudden wave of sadness. I want to run away and hide but I do not know where to go. Instead I find myself compelled to search for further reminders as if, by doing so, I am bringing her close to me, a form of nostalgic self-torture. I open a cupboard and there are her Rayne's shoes in their boxes, and hanging above them are suits and dresses, each one of which had drawn from me when she had first worn them an exclamation: 'You look lovely, darling!' Everywhere were these reminders. In another drawer were multi-coloured scarves, a pair of black mesh stockings, and a White House handkerchief with the initial 'J' in a corner. I say to myself that I ought to dispose of them, empty

166

the drawers and the cupboards, let others have the benefit of wearing them. But I am unable to make such a decision. I gain a strange comfort from my nostalgic self-torture.

I need this strange comfort to counter my confusion. It is, in a way, a tangible contact with her. It gives me the feeling that she is with me all the time. True she disappears from my mind like a cloud hiding the sun, but soon she is back again, brimming warmth into my life ... and suddenly bringing the tears. There was such an incident the other evening when I was listening to a Debussy piano recital on the radio, and the pianist was playing 'Reflets dans L'Eau', one of the pieces I had chosen when I was a castaway on Roy Plomley's *Desert Island Discs*. I remembered how I told her, when we were planning my eight records, that I used to listen to it being played on the electric piano called the Welte in my old home of Glendorgal on the cliffs near Newquay. I told her how I used to listen to it sitting in the curved window of Glendorgal, in darkness, the winking light of Trevose Head lighthouse behind me, the light which my father used to call Becky's Eye. And I would be alone, fourteen years old, listening to the music, dreaming of my future. Now I was listening to the same music, dreaming of my past.

I have moments when I am very vulnerable. Those who have suffered tragedy are aware of what I mean. One can appear to the outsider to be behaving normally. One is not looking miserable. One is not boring friends with one's sadness. One is apparently facing the loss, whether it may have been a parent, a child, a close friend, a wife or a husband, with equanimity. Unless the outsider has suffered a similar experience, they will not understand what lies beneath that equanimity. Professional counsellors, for instance, may be trained in sentences of comfort, but unless they themselves have truly suffered their counselling sentences are theoretical.

No counselling, for instance, can cure the companionship void. Jeannie and I could vent on each other our frustrations, each of us absorbing them like a sponge absorbs water, and by doing so we doused the fury of such frustrations without inflicting it on anyone who caused them. Companionship, which is the kernel of a love affair, is what I now missed above all. I had no one to lean on, no one to nudge, no one with whom to rejoice at a moment of success, no one to commiserate with when something went wrong, no one to be angry with when I was in the mood to be angry.

My vulnerability lay in the danger of addressing comparative strangers with confidences, using them as recipients as if they were Jeannie. The urge to do so sometimes spilled out of my mouth like a stream bursting its banks, and I would say things that afterwards I regretted terribly; and I would fear what the recipients of my spillage might be telling their friends. An old story, of course. How many times has one been to a party and later, lying awake at three o'clock in the morning, worried about what one had said.

My catering was not elaborate. Breakfast has always been a bore to me. I like the idea of porridge, eggs and bacon, or kidneys, or kedgeree, or slices of cold ham, all of which, and more, provided the traditional breakfast of my father's day. At Harrow, as a fag, I used to prepare such breakfasts for the prefects and their guests, usually bleary-eyed masters . . . and this is perhaps the reason why I developed an aversion to breakfast. Jeannie had the same aversion, but she has been brought up to believe that breakfast was an essential beginning to the day. Hence, whether I wanted it or not, she provided me with a breakfast, bacon and eggs usually, and the bacon often ended up with the gull on the roof. Now that I was alone, I was able to be free of breakfasts. However, there remained a breakfast itch in my mind. I was brought up to have breakfast, Jeannie urged me to have breakfast . . . and such a background made me feel I *ought* to have breakfast. Hence I compromised. I avoided a cooked breakfast; and I have instead fruit out of a tin. So easy. No tiresome half-asleep cooking. And strength provided for the morning ahead.

I have meat delivered by Datapost from a firm in Devon, fish comes from Newlyn. I order perhaps ten pounds of lemon sole at a time, and I put each fillet in a separate freezer bag. When I favour such a fillet, I do not defrost it. I place it directly into the pressure cooker, and steam it for five minutes after the knob has shown the pressure is correct. As yet I make only one sauce, a sauce with fresh parsely that I grow throughout the year in the greenhouse. In summer I serve mint with the delicious Foremost new potatoes which I also grow in the greenhouse.

I have the usual joints roasted in the usual way, but I have a speciality in the form of a pressure-cooked gammon. The gammon is unwrapped from its Datapost-sealed polythene cover and soaked in cold water for twenty-four hours. Then into the pressure cooker, three quarters filled with water, it goes, accompanied by cut-up celery, carrots, a small onion and a touch of mixed herbs. Cooking time is twelve minutes a pound. Thus a four-pound gammon is ready to serve in forty-eight minutes. So easy. And there is a bonus. I remove the gammon from the pressure cooker, pour lentils into the left behind stock . . . and thereby, after another twenty minutes cooking, I have a delicious lentil soup.

Ambrose and Cherry had their own supply corner in the freezer. There were bundles of freshly frozen ling and coley, and there was also a bundle of Ambrose's special delight, lamb's liver. They did not, however, have such items regularly on their menu. A sequence of varied cat tins was provided for them by me and I was surprised, often annoyed, by the way they sometimes turned up their noses at some brand which was being highly advertised in the media. I would open the tin, spoon it out into saucers, then find the cats gave one sniff and walked away.

It was on such occasions that Hamlet scored. Hamlet continued to come spasmodically. He might come daily for a week, then disappear for a week. I would look out of the porch window of a morning, and see him sitting a couple of yards away from the door, blinking, tip of tail curled across front paws, and I would exclaim: 'You're in luck, Hamlet! A highly advertised tin was spurned last night!' And I would fetch the saucers which hadn't been touched, empty one into the other, open the door and deposit it on the path. As I did so, Hamlet would scurry as usual beneath the *Escallonia*. He would return to gollop the spurned contents as soon as I was gone.

Sometimes, however, he appeared quite confident and he would remain in sight even when a visitor was present. On one such an occasion, a visitor made a remark which sent a shiver of apprehension through me.

'I'm sure he'll be in the cottage before long,' the woman said; adding tactlessly, 'Ambrose is old, isn't he . . . Hamlet may think there may be a vacancy.'

I could have chucked the trowel I was holding in my hand at her. I knew Ambrose was growing old but I was never going to admit it. Others, from time to time, had made the same kind of remark. Ambrose, in his new role of being friendly to strangers, might be strolling near by. 'How old is he? Getting on, isn't he?'

Ambrose was my closest companion. Sometimes I would wake up from a dream in the middle of the night, instinctively putting out an arm believing Jeannie was beside me, but it was Ambrose who was beside me. Ambrose, as always, came on strolls with me; and often, as I was standing alone, he would suddenly appear, yapping a greeting. I did not therefore want to be reminded that he was growing old, that he was thinner than he used to be, that he had lost the full shine of his bracken-coloured fur. I was pretending to be cheerful in any case, and the cheerfulness was skin deep. Such remarks made me realize that if a person is in trouble, *lift them up*. Make the person feel fine, feel good. Never yield to the temptation of pointing out a fault. Such a fault, however trivial, becomes hurtfully exaggerated in the person's mind.

Ambrose's walks with me to the Ambrose Rock had become infrequent, but this was not because of unwillingness on Ambrose's part to come with me. It was because of Susie. Susie liked to chase rabbits, liked to chase Ambrose; and as she and Merlin were often in the Oliver land field, it meant that Ambrose was denied his walk to the Ambrose Rock. He could only come with me when the donkeys were in the stable field in front of the cottage.

They were there one August early morning when I went out of the cottage, Ambrose following me. There was a thick mist full of scents as I walked down the lane, earthy scents, wild flower scents, sea scents. The flowerbeds around the cottage were looking untidy but I did not mind because I prefer a cottage garden to look untidy. I feel it is a defiant gesture against clinical gardening.

The *Alstroemeria* had finished, their tired green tendrils sprawling into the path. Climbing nasturtiums twined their way up the fuchsia bush, and fell like a waterfall from the rock beds. Busy Lizzies and mignonette looked refreshed from the night's rain. Roses had dead blooms waiting to be clipped. Bindweed was climbing everywhere. Dandelions were losing their flowers, turning into white fluffy seeds soon to fly away in a breeze. Charlie the chaffinch was shouting for crushed biscuits. Weeds were growing obstinately in the path. Brambles were stretching out, growing an inch a day. Hornbeams were thrusting up where I do not need them, ignoring the places where I do need them. Around me the scarlet of the *Montbretia*, the berries of the Rose of Sharon, swallows swimming in the sky ... and up there on the roof the raucous squawk of the Lager Louts.

Minack had been accustomed to quiet gulls. Hubert, Philip Knocker . . . all had made us aware of their presence when they considered it was time for us to feed them. They announced their arrival with short bursts of cries or, as in the case of Knocker, by knocking his beak on the glass roof of the porch. They were well mannered. They did not continue to cry greedily for more after we had thrown up on to the roof the morsels we had available. They might stay contemplating for a while, but then they would fly silently away across the moorland, dipping all the while towards the rocks and the sea. The evening gull did not even cry. He just waited patiently until I was aware of his presence.

This spring, however, two gulls arrived of a different nature. I welcomed them in friendly fashion and, as at the time I was clearing out the freezer of various items that had been there a long time, they were fortunate, after the items had defrosted, to have a feast during the following days. It was a mistake on my part. They were enchanted by this gull restaurant and, instead of treating the menu as a one-off affair, they decided to take up permanent residence at the restaurant.

The consequence has been unfortunate. I had never thought the time might come when I would possess a water pistol for the purpose of trying to drive a gull away from the roof, but that is what happened. I did not buy the toy water pistol myself. It was given to me by a schoolgirl who arrived at the cottage one day at the moment I was shouting at the two gulls: 'Go away! Go away! You've been here squawking since dawn . . . go and do some work, you Lager Louts! Go and get your own food, plenty of fish in the sea!' I apologized to the girl, explaining the reason for my behaviour; and the following morning she returned with the water pistol.

It was ineffective. The spurt of water never reached the top of the roof. The gulls stayed, and I continued to yell at them. They arrived at dawn and, if I was awake, I would hear them chatting their way up the valley from the rocks until they landed on the roof with a screech. I did not understand their way of thinking. At that hour there was not a chance of them having any food, and one would have thought, this lesson learnt, that they would change their tactics. Not a bit of it. They preferred to stay all day, sometimes screeching, sometimes mewing a burbling sound like an orchestra tuning up. There was another reason for their unpopularity. The evening gull, the gentle, silent, shy evening gull, would float up from the sea as dusk was falling, to find the Lager Louts still hogging the roof.

Ambrose and I continued our early morning stroll down the lane, past the white seat with the burgeoning honeysuckle which filled the air with its scent as we passed; and a few yards further on there was another scent, the sweet, exotic scent of the leaves of the *Trichocarpa* tree. Then on we went to Monty's Leap, Ambrose taking the plank at the side to cross, and on up the lane to the gate which leads to Oliver land. Ambrose was keen for this stroll, I could see that. There were no pauses, no hanging around sniffing at tufts of grass, no alerts for possible mice.

Ambrose was coming with me as if he knew very well where we were going.

We reached the Ambrose Rock and I heaved myself up on it, and a second later Ambrose had jumped beside me, and we sat there, my legs dangling above the green grass while Ambrose began a *sotto voce* purr which gradually turned into a *crescendo*. The mist was lifting, and there was no longer a veil over Carn Barges; and looking back to the cottage I could see the Lager Louts on the roof. I sat there pondering about my future, just as Jeannie and I had sat there thinking about *our* future.

The realization had slowly been seeping into me that I was a bachelor again. It was as if I was again in my mews cottage off London's King's Road or in the now demolished Ackers Street in Manchester, or on my journey round the world, or writing the story of that journey, *Time Was Mine*, in the ancient cottage near Truro. My life with Jeannie was now only a dream.

I would not marry again. I knew that. Yet I would be needing feminine companionship. I would be looking for a girl like Jeannie, as I looked for a Jeannie those years ago. I would look, as I did then, for a girl who flinted my mind, someone whose companionship, at whatever distance, would be stimulating. A gentle person. A girl with whom I could always flirt as if we had just met, just as I did all the time with Jeannie. A girl who intuitively shared the hopes and philosophy of life that I had. A girl who was vulnerable. A girl who had the courage to keep her individuality. A girl who could laugh easily. A girl who found excitement in small pleasures. A girl whose knowledge of literature and music was not that of an intellectual, but that of a romantic who secured comfort from them as an antidote to the rush of her life. Jeannie had all of this, and much more . . . but the reality of that time was over. I was a bachelor again.

Ambrose, beside me, was still purring. The *crescendo* had moderated to a soft purr, a contented, 'Don't disturb me' purr; and all the while the morning mist was continuing to lift, and the sun had begun to appear over Mount's Bay shaped as the sun, but as yet no dazzling light.

I sat there pondering about the time of my first bachelorhood, remembering incidents, remembering lessons learnt. The dreariness that followed the end of a love affair by the thought of the small talk which would have to inaugurate another. The shyness I felt, the disbelief that a girl was responding. The ability to be dashing with a girl I didn't care for, but dumb with the girl I did. The flick of mutual attraction with a girl in a bus, a tube, in a restaurant, whom I was never to meet. The glorious dawn of a love affair when each is trying to discover the other. Then the ending, embers flickering, when one says to the other: 'I know everything about you' – the signal that the affair is dying; the lesson thus learnt that mystery sustains romance. In those days of my first bachelorhood I remember observing the failures of marriage, the sight of a bored married couple, as if they were locked together in a cage. I remember my moods . . . yearning for a special girl so much that I found comfort just by looking at a map, and finding the street in which she lived. I remember the problem of tactics: shall I ignore her, or shall I send her flowers? Should I telephone her or keep silent? Some love affairs have the brilliance of a butterfly's short summer of joy. So easy. No complications. So quickly over. Exquisite is the love affair when the two of you are so in tune that you interchange the smallest details of a day's activity. Companionship, rather than desire, is the kernel of a love affair. End a love affair, I remember being told, with grace.

These thoughts flitting through my mind, Ambrose beside me, were balanced by the awareness that I was thinking of the remembrances of things past. In those exploring days there was always the motivation that I was seeking a Jeannie. Now I could only look forward to stepping stones leading me nowhere. I was not, however, as despondent as I sound. The stepping stones might prove delightful. Jeannie would be glad.

I sat there thinking of the Minack Chronicles Trust, and how lucky I was to have such Trustees whom I knew would care for it, whatever might happen to me. The final terms were still to be drafted, and I was needing expert help, but in the meantime a legal document had been signed which covered emergencies.

True it was a very small part of Cornwall which was being preserved for posterity, but the need for such efforts to preserve has become even more imperative than when Jeannie and I first thought of forming the Trust. Millionaire entrepreneurs have descended upon Cornwall, attracted by the commercial possibilities of exploiting its mystery, its away-from-the-rat-race atmosphere; and they fly in their privately owned helicopters, glancing down at the landscape and seashore, calculating where development would be most profitable.

'Cornwall has such potential it is unbelievable,' said one famous entrepreneur, 'when you think how people are falling over themselves in the south-east for a tiny parcel of development. Cornwall is a gold-mine.'

The entrepreneurs dazzle local dignitaries with their *bonhomie*, their hospitable press conferences and their promises of job creation in the area should their plans be approved. Intuitively many of those who are courted sense that the proposed plans are not in the true interest of Cornwall. But, in this materialistic world in which profit rather than service is the predominant factor, the local authorities are in a dilemma. The loners, the dreamers, those who truly sense the magic of Cornwall are in the minority. They cannot compete, in money terms, with the computer assessment of the money that might be brought into the county by the plastic society. Hence local authorities are pressurized, bit by bit, to surrender the notion that Cornwall is a world apart from the rest of the country, a maverick of a county. Cornwall must conform. Cornwall must lose its mystery.

But there is another danger to Cornwall, a graver one, and it is the consequence of exploitation. Instead of the leisurely attitude of trust and friendliness, the harsh realities of material progress will have to be faced. The urban, up-country pace of life will be adopted. Fear will creep into Cornwall.

'Is it safe to walk the coastal path alone?' I have been asked by city holidaymakers.

'Of course!' I have replied, laughing.

Their question, however, mirrors the mood in which many people now live, the mood which will come to Cornwall if the developers have their way. Can they be prevented? I doubt it. They can only be checked. The United Kingdom is vastly overpopulated. The demand to turn green fields into cement will ever increase; and by so doing the ethical values of life will deteriorate. Cornwall will no longer be a harbour of tranquillity.

There are those, of course, who are fighting this rape of Cornwall, and one of the groups is the Cornwall Trust for Nature Conservation. It is a dedicated organization, maintained by public subscription, and helped by voluntary workers. It issues regular bulletins describing its efforts. It has acquired its own nature reserves, bought out of public subscription; and it is the enemy of the ruthless developer. The Minack Chronicles Trust, it is planned, will liaise closely with it.

Meanwhile, on my local scene, the end of an era was in progress. Years ago, Jack Cockram, employed as a worker of a nearby farm where he had been evacuated as a child from a wartime bombed London, stopped me as I was driving along the lane to the main road, and asked me if I had any influence which might help him to become tenant of the farm at the top of the Minack lane which was soon to become vacant. Jack did not need my influence. The landlord's agent realised his quality, and assigned him the farm.

He came to the farm, amalgamated with the adjacent farm of Walter Grose, had two daughters both of whom were to have brilliant careers, and, from the moment of their arrival, remained, with his wife Alice, the special friends of Jeannie and myself. Now, with a flick of the page, their story was over. The daughters had flown away, farming costs had risen and ill health had had its influence. They had been such good neighbours. Their successors no doubt would be too. But a style of farming would end when Jack and Walter left. They kept to the standards of husbandry which belonged to the time when wages were low so that non-productive aspects of farming could be maintained. On the farm of today there is a hectic, tractor-rushing activity which resembles traffic in a busy city centre. I have seen Walter Grose hoeing a five-acre field. Part of history. Soothing, beautiful and environmentally safer than the tractor's roar and the tractor's spraying of weedkillers and insecticide. Now the time of Jack and Walter, Walter the Pied Piper of cats because of the many he had collected, was over. I would no longer have the calm comfort of seeing them, making ageless remarks about the weather, about the crops, or having the chance to say to eighty-year-old Walter, digging the ditch at the side of Minack lane: 'Why are you doing that, Walter? It's my job to do that!'

And that answer of his, Walter who loved Jeannie: 'I'm doing it for *her*.'

No longer would Jack bring me a bundle of carrots or a basket of peas saying with a smile: 'Penance!' . . . and by 'penance' he meant he was apologizing for the escape of his cattle into our fields during the day before. Nor would I have the comfort of Jack bringing out his tractor, cheerfully, despite great inconveni-

ence, to pull out a visitor's car which had skidded
into the ditch. Or just asking what help he could
give, now that I was on my own. We had been at ease
with these two. Jeannie used to walk up the lane to
the farm to collect the milk, rich milk which she
would turn into real Cornish clotted cream; and Jack
would hang the container on a hook outside the
farmhouse for her to collect. Such lovely cream she
used to make. She would not be able to make it now.
There is a law stopping people from buying non-
pasteurized milk from farms. The law has resulted in
real Cornish cream becoming a distant memory. The
Cornish cream of today, made from pasteurized milk
and sold in shops as Cornish cream, is a mockery of
real Cornish cream. We had been at ease with these
two, Jack and Walter, and sweet Alice, Jack's wife.
Now the end had come.

There was another change. The landlord had auc-
tioned an ancient, derelict cottage in the centre of the
farm complex, a complex which had been occupied
by Cornish people since the beginning of time; and it
was bought by a developer. In a few weeks of day
and night work, he had converted it into a holiday
home which he proceeded to sell.

Jack and Walter handed over the farm to the in-
coming tenants on Michaelmas Day. A fortnight
before, they had the customary end-of-tenancy farm
sale which included, of course, their herd of Friesian
steers. I could see the sale taking place in a field near
the farm but I did not go. Such sales, I find, are sad
occasions; and there was one special reason why I did
not go.

A week previously I looked out of the bedroom

window, and saw what I momentarily thought was the black roof of a stationary car. A second later I realized my mistake. It wasn't a car. It was a steer, and I recognized the black coat with white markings as that of the steer which Jeannie and I called the king of the herd. He was a magnificent animal, dwarfing the rest of the herd; and we often admired him as he grazed in any field near the cottage. We had other reasons to take notice of him. On occasions when he and his companions broke out of their field into one of our fields, the king would come face to face with Fred and Merlin. Fred would stand his ground, Merlin would flee. Fred would resemble a stag at bay and we would shout: 'Bravo Fred!' But there was also another side to the relationship between the two. Often they would appear to be talking to each other in friendly fashion, nose to nose, over the hedge. The king, we felt, was a friendly steer.

Now he was outside the bedroom window a week before the sale where he would be sold at an auction, leading to an inevitable future. He stood there pensively, so unlike the usual behaviour of a steer which has escaped from a field. No sign of fright. It was as if he had come to say goodbye, as if he was remembering the times he had enjoyed grazing around Minack. It was uncanny. I did not disturb him. I am sure he did not know that I was there. I just watched as he slowly ambled down to the stable meadow gate beside the barn. He looked over the gate for a minute, then he turned round, lumbered past the cherry tree to the white seat, where he paused again, looked towards the cottage, then slowly went away up the lane, across Monty's Leap, and back up the hill to the farm. I was very moved. It wasn't the ordinary visit of an escaping steer.

On the day of the sale the post had arrived with a letter from my publisher. A few days before I had despatched the *Jeannie* manuscript by the British Railways Red Star service. I nervously picked up the envelope, hesitated, decided to delay opening it for a minute or two by filling and lighting a pipe. Then I settled down on the sofa, the sofa which had been a part of my life since pre-war London days, only to find that I had left my spectacles on my desk. I got up and fetched them, settled down again, and read the following:

I find it hard to express my feelings having finished *Jeannie* [wrote my publisher]. Reading it has been an intensely emotional experience. You have wonderfully captured Jeannie's joyous and generous spirit . . . She leaps off the page with such vivacity that it is easy to picture her still at Minack. It is, literally, a triumph of life over death.

I sat there, the letter in my hands . . . and I looked across at the chair where Jeannie always sat, an armchair opposite me.

I saw her smiling.

XI

23 March ... two years since Jeannie's memorial service.

Sister Catherine from St Michael's Hospital, Hayle, had come to see me. Jeannie had loved her. Sister Catherine belonged to the Roman Catholic Order of the Daughters of the Cross of Liege. This Order organizes the very caring St Michael's Hospital.

'It was her smile,' Sister Catherine said to me. She was with Jeannie at the end. 'The whole room would light up when she smiled, and however ill she may have been feeling, she still greeted you with this smile. Yes, she was ageless, so very young she looked. A hospital porter said to me: "That's a pretty Miss you have in 207" ... and although she may have thought she was dying, she disclosed this to none of us.'

She never disclosed it to me and, for my part, I do not think she believed she was dying. There was, therefore, no organized farewell, and this I find comforting. It makes dying an ordinary, everyday affair, making it so natural an event, that the shock of it is softened. I mean that in some curious way one feels that it has never happened, and that life will continue, although the body will be absent; and because there was no final farewell, I feel that Jeannie has never left me.

I dream of her quite often (and as I write the words, the melody is in my mind of 'I Dream of Jeannie with the Light Brown Hair'); and the dream, a recurring one with variations, centres on hotels rather than Minack. I will go, for instance, to a hotel to meet Jeannie, a nameless elegant London hotel, and she is not there. I wait and wait, a message comes, and it comes through her fascinating voice, and she is telling me that she is busy. Last night had a variation of the dream. I was in a luxurious suite on the first floor of Claridge's, alone. Then the phone rang, and it was Jeannie, and she said she was in the neighbouring suite, and before I could ask her why she was not sharing mine, she said: 'You've run out of razor blades . . . I've got one for you.'

I had, in reality, run out of razor blades.

Hamlet had gone missing a few weeks before Christmas. At first I took his absence as a natural event, taking it for granted that he had changed his mind about taking up residence at Minack. I missed his spasmodic visits, but at the same time I was relieved. Cherry would no longer be threatened, and there would be no prospect of Ambrose's comfortable routine being upset. For I was becoming worried about Ambrose. His appetite was good, he was active, but he looked thin.

After Hamlet's absence for three or four weeks I went and saw Dora and John Phillips who have a farm not far away, and who are hosts to a multitude of cats. Cats of many varied colours, cats of all ages, cats who fill the chairs, cats nursing baskets of kittens, cats queuing for the food which is liberally provided for them by Dora. I told them of my experience with Hamlet during the summer and autumn months, and Dora replied that he used to come and see them too. 'Dash into the kitchen,' she said, 'have something to eat, and dash away again. He never stayed.' Then she added, 'We haven't seen him for weeks.'

It was a while later that I got nearer to the truth as to what happened to him. I met a couple who had a cottage not far from the Phillips's farm. They told me a black cat, and no doubt it was Hamlet, used to visit them from time to time and one day he came hobbling on three legs, holding the paw of his other leg well above the ground. He did not look well, they said; and they never saw him again. Poor Hamlet, he seemed to want love, seemed to want to free himself from his loneliness . . . but he was afraid to commit himself.

23 March . . . it is such a joyous time of year, the daffodils ablaze in the meadows, row upon row upon row of them, ribbons of yellow, and when I looked at them I felt nostalgic, thinking of all those early mornings and the dying lights of evening, when Jeannie and I would be desperately picking their forebears, picking with the left hand, passing them to the right when the left hand could take no more then, when the right hand was full, dropping the unsorted bundle to the ground. There they would lie until the picking was finished, and I would proceed to collect them, placing them in a barrel of a wicker basket, then collecting the tractor, heaving the baskets into the carrier, and driving back to the cottage and the packing house.

'A lovely picking,' Jeannie would say happily.

At present there was no picking; the daffodils remained where they should always belong. No dustbins for them. Jeannie would be pleased. She only mentioned 'a lovely picking' because at the time we were seeking financial survival.

There come times in all our lives when depression sweeps over us, when some incident, a let-down perhaps, causes great distress. One is inclined to yearn on such occasions to confide in a person one can trust but it is often hard to find such a person. One needs a person upon whom one can completely rely to keep one's emotions secret. For myself, however, I struggle to keep silent, and wait for my emotions to subside. Or, of course, I may use Ambrose or Merlin or Cherry as the receptacle of my secret thoughts.

There was one person, however, whom Jeannie and I could always rely upon, and that was Canon Martin Andrews; and, since Jeannie's death, when I have been feeling low I have gone to a call box and talked to him. In a few minutes he would restore balance to my outlook; and this was due to himself having witnessed much sadness, and he was an example as to how to cope with it.

He also mirrored the belief I have that, in terms of personal relationships, age need not matter. It is sharing the same wavelength that matters. That marvellous feeling of being at ease with the other, words flowing, the mind open. It can happen with a stranger. It may never happen with somebody close, a relation for instance. It may happen with a child of ten but never with a person of your own age. Years have no meaning when a wavelength is shared.

Jeannie and I felt in this way about Martin Andrews. He had his first book *Canon's Folly* published when he was nearly ninety. He completed his second book *Canon's Final Folly* when he was one hundred and one. He asked me to write the introduction, and this is what I said:

All of us who know Canon Andrews have had our lives enhanced by experiencing his compassion, his courage, his humour, his loving kindness . . . and his gusto.

I talked to him a while ago on the telephone from a call box. On hearing my voice, he boomed: 'Didn't I tell you last time, dearie, to *reverse the charges*?'

And there was the day when I asked how he had enjoyed living on his own in his Downderry home (he was over one hundred years old) . . . and he replied, his voice again booming over the telephone: 'Marvellous, dearie . . . I can make a damned fool of myself without anyone knowing!'

He was, in relation terms, second cousin to Jeannie, although she always referred to him as Uncle Martin. He had been a close friend of her father's, and he was to become a very close friend of Jeannie. He adored her, and she adored him. I remember her saying one day when we were on our way to see him (Jeannie with smoked salmon, which is his culinary weakness, and a bone for Honey his beloved Golden Labrador), how wonderful it was to be on the same wavelength with someone so much older.

All who know him are aware that he is a very humble person. He is always wondering why people love him. I said to him once I believed it was partly due to people feeling safe with him. They can unload their secret thoughts without fear he would ever pass them on to others. The Duke of Windsor certainly felt this. He unburdened his secret thoughts to Martin during the great crisis of his life . . . and these thoughts remained secret.

In this book he reflects on the Abdication crisis, and the emotional agony of those involved, and he does so in a very delicate and revealing manner. He sensitively conveys his own impressions of his meetings with the Duke, then Prince of Wales, without disclosing any intimacies. So too with his anecdotes of other members of the Royal Family.

There is the story of the Queen Mother and the cabbage. She came, when Queen, with King George VI for lunch with Martin at Stoke Climsland Rectory. At the last moment of preparation, the garden beans were found to be stringy. The only alternative was to serve cabbage.

'Oh how wonderful!' exclaimed the Queen when it was served. 'Nobody ever gives us cabbage!'

Martin calls everyone 'dearie'. At his hundredth birthday party, I heard him laughingly say to a middle-aged gentleman who had been one of his parishioners: 'I christened you, dearie, I married you, and who knows I may bury you, dearie!' Jeannie and I, on a visit to him, found him pottering in the little greenhouse tending the geraniums he loves to grow.

'Have this,' said Martin, handing Jeannie a little pot containing a seedling, 'I bred it myself.'

'What is it called?' she asked, thanking him.

'Dearie,' he replied. And we all laughed.

His ninetieth birthday had also been celebrated by a lavish party, organized by a one-time Australian airman, Peter Stafford, who was one of the many Australian airman who were given a peaceful harbour at Stoke Climsland when on leave during the Hitler war years. Like others he had never forgotten the kindness and comfort Martin had given him, nor that of Vincent Curtis.

Vincent had been with Martin since a boy, and used to manage the market garden at Stoke Climsland which Martin had begun with the backing of the Prince of Wales soon after the First World War. Vincent was a man of many gifts, a wonderful companion, and a true friend. Peter Stafford, meanwhile, had become a distinguished hotelier, and at the time of Martin's party was general manager of the Dorchester.

A gale began to stir on the night of the celebration. A marquee had been installed on the lawn at Downderry to where Martin had moved after he retired; and as the gale grew fiercer and fiercer, the sides began wildly to flap and the canvas top heave.

'It's going to take off any moment,' said one guest cheerfully.

It didn't. The party went on into the night, and the ninety-year-old roamed among his guests, greeting each one with: 'Are you enjoying yourself, dearie?'

He certainly enjoyed himself; and when at last Jeannie and I said goodbye to him, he expressed his happiness in a way that I will always remember.

'Good night, dearies . . .' Then he added as if it was a hallelujah: 'JOY BELLS! JOY BELLS!'

I felt, while I was reading *Canon's Final Folly*, that I was sitting in the lovely drawing room of his Downderry home, listening to him talk. It is that kind of book, a gentle book, a book of philosophy and wise words, a book that spans a hundred years of history, written by a man who is over a hundred years himself, a book of compassion.

Compassion threads through every page, compassion for the unemployed, compassion for the war-wounded and the killed, compassion for all those in distress . . . and compassion for animals.

He writes how, in his old age, he has become obsessed by the thought of animals which suffer from human exploitation. And he makes a practical suggestion:

'Why not set aside a day on which to remember suffering animals . . . and call it "Forget

Me Not Day", the flower symbolic of friendship?

'We should have the surprise of our lives at the number of people who would join in a concerted effort to raise funds for them.'

Then he adds:

'If a Forget Me Not Day for animals could be established, then this book would not have been written in vain.'

I specially remember the day of his 100th birthday. It was the first time I had been to a party without Jeannie. I felt very strange. We always separated at a party – a couple clinging together is depressing – and I found myself looking round the crowded room and thinking how, if Jeannie had been there, I would have looked across the room and seen her in the centre of an animated group, and how I would feel proud of her at the way she mixed with people so easily.

Martin died six months after he was 101. I talked to him the week before. 'How are you, dearie? Take care of yourself,' were the last words he spoke to me.

At the funeral there was a wreath from the Queen and a wreath from the Queen Mother with a special message in her own handwriting. The Bishop of Truro gave the address and, although he had never known Martin, he had done his homework, and the address was impressive. Later I had a talk with the Bishop, a very charming man, and he said, a note of question in his voice: 'He wasn't a very spiritual man, I believe.' And I replied: 'It depends what you mean as spiritual . . . he faced the reality of life. He saw no value in arguing about whether a comma should be here or there in the prayer book.'

Well meant, soothing words were often said to me as time went by; and they revolved around the belief that Jeannie would be there waiting for me when my time came. Unfortunately I have always had doubts about such a belief. There are so many imponderables. For instance, what happens to those who have had two, three, four loves? A man may always remember the teenager he loved but who died young. He may have lived happily afterwards with another he loved . . . who will he choose when he joins them?

I take comfort, however, in my belief that those who die try to keep contact with those they have left behind by a subtle form of communication. It is not in the form of spiritualism. Spiritualists are an exclusive group but, for some personal reason, I am scared of being involved. Contact with people exists, I accept that, but the idea of this is unsettling. Sometimes I wonder whether spiritualism will become a commercial project. A tycoon may see the possibilities; and then there will be a Stock Exchange boom in 'Other World' commodity shares.

I sense instead that those who have gone proceed to make their presence felt by using 'vehicles'. Such a 'vehicle' can appear in a vast variety of ways. It may, perhaps, come in the form of beauty. One is in despair but suddenly one sees a rose so perfect that it exudes an intensity of feeling which is like a message of hope; or one may be uplifted by the sight of the first swallow of spring skimming over one's home; or a sensitive letter unexpectedly arrives at the beginning of what had threatened to be a down day; or a stranger calls who, by their manner, doesn't seem a stranger, and one is taken out of one's despondency; or, in a funny case that from time to time happens to me, there is a sudden appearance of Cherry as dusk falls, and she jumps on my lap as I sit on the sofa, suddenly reminding me that I had forgotten to feed the evening gull. Will he still be there? I dump Cherry and go outside, and he is up there on the apex of the roof, turning his head as is his custom nervously, in quick succession to the left and to the right. I am glad that Cherry reminded me. Or was it Jeannie?

Ambrose, that late March, was fading. Joan, who always looked after him at any brief time when I was away, recognized this too; and, when she came on Mondays, she would bring fish for him, fish which her own cats would have loved. It was soothing to have her sharing my concern, anxiously asking when she arrived, 'How is he?'

There was another person who also shared the anxiety, and she, I have always believed, provided an instance of Jeannie's subtle influence. The girl, and I call her M., had written to me from London saying that she liked my books and intended to visit me. Her intention was to arrive at Penzance on a Friday in early May, and return to London on the Sunday, hopefully finding me at Minack on the Saturday. She was in much doubt about making this special journey but her husband told her it was about time she made a decision on her own, and did something on her own. Hence she came to Penzance, and instead of leaving the station in a taxi to take her to the Lamorna Cove Hotel, she found me waiting at the entrance to the station. 'Are you M.?' I said instinctively, when a fair girl in blue jeans holding a large canvas carrier bag appeared; and she said 'yes', and from that moment we were both so unselfconsciously at ease with each other that I felt I was with a Jeannie again.

M. was to be with me a year later, when Ambrose was fading. The only enduring quality between two people is that of enjoying a sensitive companionship. Nothing else matters. The sheer joy of sharing each other's lives and, as I once wrote, 'the exquisite pleasure of being understood without laboriously having to explain' . . . such a pleasure is a precious experience. No tedious complications. Just the ease of two sharing minds.

A few days after M. returned to London, I had to make a brief visit to London myself in connection with the coming publication of *Jeannie*. I was hesitant about going, and obviously I was prepared to cancel it if Ambrose gave me a special reason for concern. However, he had picked up during the previous couple of weeks, his appetite was good, provided the fish or ox liver, or whatever else he fancied, was well mashed; and he used happily to go wandering, enjoying momentary excitements of hunting potential mice in the tussocks of grass around the cottage, and along the side of the winding lane.

But it was not a captured mouse that decided me it was safe to leave him. It was a rabbit that did so. I was lying in bed one morning, a mug of tea in my hand, propped up by a pillow so that I could watch the donkeys nibbling grass on the other side of the shallow valley in Oliver land, when through the window appeared Ambrose heaving a rabbit, fortunately dead, and which was dangling from his mouth.

'Bravo, Ambrose!' I called out, thrilled that he was well enough to have had such a success. Ambrose had spent many hundreds of hours in his life watching rabbit holes, waiting for a rabbit to appear. I was sorry for the rabbits, but I consoled myself that, like other aspects of nature, it was nature's method of controlling nature. So different from man's obsession with destroying nature for materialistic gain.

It was, however, to prove the last rabbit he ever caught. I returned from London, a taxi bringing me from Penzance station to the cottage, and I hurried up the path to the door, slotted the Yale key into the lock, calling out all the time: 'Ambrose! Ambrose! . . . I'm home!' And I also called out what Jeannie so often called him: 'Am . . . Ambers . . . Am . . . where are you?'

I could not find him at first. There was a half-eaten plate of fish in the usual place; and then Cherry appeared from the bedroom. Cherry was very cheerful. She rubbed against my leg. Purred loudly. She was giving me a lovely welcome.

'Where's Ambrose?' I asked, speaking really to myself, not to her.

She went on purring, went on rubbing against my leg.

I looked around. Then I went up to my Regency desk, and looked down on the carpet below where it adjoins the Heatstore . . . and there was Ambrose. A favourite place, warm, pleasant to huddle against. I was so relieved. His possible disappearance towards the end of his life had always haunted me. It is understandable. The sudden disappearance of an animal, followed by fruitless searching, is an emotional agony which one can live with for ever.

Ambrose was sound asleep. He had not heard my arrival.

'Ambrose!' I exclaimed.

He stirred, opened an eye, shifted his body, a pause . . . and I swear he smiled.

A week later, 29 April, I woke up at three in the morning. I woke up scared. Ambrose wasn't on the bed as he had been during the previous nights. I got up, and found it was a false alarm. He was asleep on the sofa, and what brought further ease to my mind was that the fish I had left on a plate had all been eaten. Cherry may have had her share, but there were two plates of fish, and each was empty.

In the morning I found that the exhaust pipe of the Volvo had cracked, and so I decided to take the car into Penzance to be repaired. A snap decision. Better to have it done quickly or I would become victim to the 'put-it-off' attitude. Once in Penzance I called in to see Paul, the vet, and asked him to come and give Ambrose another check.

I arrived back at the cottage, and Ambrose was outside, sitting beside the waterbutt, in that upright cat position with tail across the paws. He moved towards me as I walked up the path, and I said: 'Wanting a walk?'

I turned then, went past the cherry tree on my right, the white seat on my left, past the stable building, past the exotic-scented *Trichocarpa*, past the domed entrance to the little well which former inhabitants of Minack had only used in winter because in summer it is dry, past the crab apple tree beside it, then on to Monty's Leap . . . and all the while Ambrose was coming slowly behind me. He stopped at the Leap, no question of him jumping over it, and I thought of the time when Oliver first carried him across it, up the lane, and into the cardboard box in the garage. We stayed there for a few minutes, Ambrose very still; and my mind returned to the memory of Monty, how we watched him on his last walk down the lane to the Leap; and me saying to Jeannie: 'Such an old warrior.' Both cats the colour of autumn bracken.

It was to be Ambrose's last walk. I carried him back in my arms to the cottage. He died next morning.

Joan came that afternoon, and set about tidying the cottage because, she said, at this of all times I would not be happy in an untidy cottage. She loved Ambrose so much, had done so much to care for him during the past few months.

In the evening I rang M. in London from the call box at Sparnon, near St Buryan, a call box which once won nationwide fame as the call box best cared for by the lady responsible for its appearance. I was seeking to talk to someone who would understand how I was feeling. It was like talking to Jeannie. M. immediately said that, if I would like her to, she would come down on the Sunday, and go back on the Monday night train. She and her husband were flying abroad later in the week, but she insisted she could manage such a visit, and I said it would be a very special help.

I asked Tom Harvey, my friend the carpenter, to

make a special box; and Mike, my friend at Rosmodres, said he would dig the pit in the honeysuckle meadow, sparing me the work. So all was ready when M. arrived. It was cold that Sunday afternoon, a near gale blowing; and M. had to cope with me sitting in front of the fire talking about the past with Ambrose. It was a gentle part of her character that she understood. I needed her understanding, and yet she was doubtful. 'You *did* want me to come, didn't you? You're sure?' she had asked.

She brought from London a red geranium in a pot, as a memory to Ambrose. It is still beside me as I write.

We buried him in the evening of Monday, a cloudy, stormy evening, rain on the way. I could not carry the little basket in which Ambrose temporarily lay because I had the shovel, the screwdriver to fasten down the box, and a jersey which Jeannie used to wear, upon which I intended to lay Ambrose.

M. carried the little basket instead and, on looking back, I saw her stooping every now and again. She was picking wild flowers, a wild violet, a bluebell, a celandine, the tip of a pink campion, a white petal of blackthorn, and was dropping them around Ambrose in his little basket.

We buried him close to where Oliver lay, beneath the ancient Cornish hedge which is at the back of the honeysuckle meadow. It was very quiet except for the sound of the wind and the sea; and I placed beside him in his box a copy of *The Ambrose Rock*, in which I had written: 'Ambrose . . . our beloved friend from the moment he appeared from the bracken above Monty's Leap.'

Then M. and I stood there, silent, looking out across the moorland to Carn Barges and the expanse of Mount's Bay, both of us aware of a very special moment.

Then, in the distance, I heard the faint chugging engine of the *Scillonian* on her way back from the Scillies to Penzance.

'The *Scillonian* is coming,' I murmured.

'I can't hear it,' said M., adding, 'but you're used to the sound all through the year.'

The *Scillonian* came into view, white horses of the waves as escort; past the Bucks, past the cliff meadows where Jeannie, bent double, had picked so many flowers, picked up so many new potatoes; and now she was heaving in the sea in front of us, the yellow of the gorse framing her; then to Carn Barges, nosing past close enough for us to see only her mast as she passed. Away then, out of sight, past Lamorna Cove, past Carn Dhu, past Mousehole, on the way to Penzance Harbour.

Ambrose.

I stood there remembering the lines which Jeannie had written:

> The spirits of Minack
> Welcome you
> To their world of Forever
> Where life continues
> And death is never.

XII

Three years since Jeannie's memorial service.

I wish I could believe in the philosophy that time heals. It depends, I suppose, on the depth of the wound that has to be healed. A shallow cut, and the healing is quick. A deep cut, and the scar remains. It is the same for all those who have lost someone they have loved. There will always be moments waiting to pounce, bringing back the pain, bringing back the vacuum.

I am lucky because I live in a world of natural beauty; and every blade of grass, every inch of soil, every ancient rock offers me the security of knowing that my roots are here, so giving me comfort. I am lucky also to have a motivation for my life. I will be fulfilling Jeannie's dream if I succeed in making watertight the future of Oliver land, and of Minack, safe from any philistine developer. The Minack Chronicle Trust is ready to take over if I were to be run over by a bus, but there are still imponderables to consider.

There is another aspect to the Trust, apart from its basic conception. Jeannie and I agreed that the Trust need not solely deal with Oliver land. The running costs of looking after Oliver land should not be excessive. Hence we decided that the Trustees, at their discretion, should be free to contribute to the preservation of other parts of Cornwall, should the funds be available. Always, however, the purpose will be to preserve *wild* Cornwall. We had become aware that amusement-park-type developers are as much a threat to *wild* Cornwall as building developers . . . for they set out, in the pursuit of materialism, to destroy the soul of Cornwall.

I am still faced with the problem of preserving Minack itself, and the surrounding twenty acres, though, as a tenant, it is presumptuous for me to consider it my task to do so. Yet, because we have lived here for many years, have been allowed by the landlord to live here undisturbed, it is understandable that we came to love Minack as if we owned it. Nonetheless the landlord has to view his financial investments in a broad context. Hence Minack may one day be vulnerable. Someone might move in, ignorant of its history, not caring, and turn it into a stockbroker-belt-type holiday home. The simplicity of Minack, the simplicity of antiquity, would then die.

I was intrigued, therefore, by a visit last summer by an Inspector of the Department of the Environment English Heritage Division. His purpose was to make a preliminary assessment as to whether Minack should be listed in the Historic Buildings of England Survey. The Inspector was well acquainted with the Minack Chronicles, and he said that their reputation would help the choice of Minack being included in the Survey. In that event Minack would have a form of legal protection against any developer for all time.

The Inspector explained that there would be further inspections by the Department, and a full report drawn up before a decision was made.

After he had left I suffered one of those moments which are waiting to pounce. Jeannie would have celebrated, although there was nothing yet to celebrate. She was such fun.

In due course there were other inspections, and photographs were taken of the cottage, and of the stables where the donkeys have mincepies on Christmas Eve. I pointed out the cobblestone floor, the long ago substitute for cement, and more photographs were taken. Then silence. No word came as to the result of the Department's deliberations. There is still silence.

Meanwhile the Lager Louts had gone absent this spring. Quiet reigned on the roof for the time being, no greedy cries, no early morning squawking reveille; and the evening gull was back on his own again. Perversely I missed the Lager Louts. True, they represented in my mind the unthinking hooligans of society, whereas the evening gull represented all those who seek peace in solitude, yet they had flattered me by their attention. It was a pleasant thought that they depended on Minack.

Cherry did not grieve for Ambrose, although on that afternoon we buried him she behaved in a most unexpected manner. She followed us as we went up the lane, then, to my surprise, she then followed us into Oliver land. She started to cross it with us, hesitantly because of the donkeys. Half-way Susie caught sight of her, and began to chase her . . . and Cherry raced first to the far hedge, then switched round and raced back to the lane, Susie after her. It was a near thing.

Later, when we came back to the field, she was there again, further down in the field, a little black crouching figure. It was as if she was determined to be with us as we said goodbye to Ambrose. 'Cherry has come of age today,' said M.

But Cherry didn't grieve, no doubt because of the division which had always existed between her and Ambrose. She was puzzled by his absence, sometimes wandered around as if she were looking for him, expecting him suddenly to appear; but she was soon to take over Ambrose's role towards me. She was soon to become my confidante.

She was soon able to pursue those antics aimed to charm a one-time reluctant cat-lover like myself. She felt uninhibited. No Ambrose to rival her. When I went to the spare room to write, it would not be long before she jumped upon the table beside me, wishing to play with the keys of the typewriter, mystified when my finger touched a letter and the letter bounced up and hit an outstretched paw. What does one do? Stop typing? Stop searching one's mind for the words to write? Play with her? Of course play with her.

As always it was the sofa, the settee, which posed the most serious problem. A place to relax, to pick up a book, re-read a letter, to ruminate, a drink in one's hand, a Prestige pressure-cooker supper softly hissing on the stove . . . then up jumps Cherry on my lap. If only cats could be trained to fetch a drink, to turn off the stove; but there is Cherry on my lap, purring, dribbling in ecstasy, an example of the peace of mind we all want to achieve. I want my supper! How can I move? Dare I move? Suddenly the bell of the pressure cooker rings. The meal is ready. 'Sorry Cherry,' I say in a Uriah Heep tone, 'I must push you off.'

Her endearing trait is that she cannot miaow. She opens her little mouth as if to make a sound, but no sound materializes, except a tiny squeak. Heaven knows what would happen if she was in trouble. Ambrose would have bellowed. But Cherry, sweet, loving Cherry, is a mute. She represents love without artifice, and therefore she always has a soothing influence on me. She gives me so much that I do not begrudge her own demands on me. Hence I do not mind when my legs get cramp, my glass is empty, my supper is overcooked. I am living in a world which has not been brainwashed by surface pleasure, or by logic. I am just being happy in the company of a cat.

This spring the grass was lush after the heavy rain of the winter. Lush grass in spring and early summer poses a threat to donkeys. Too much rich grass and laminitis threatens, an inflammation of the feet which can easily become chronic. I have always been on guard against it, always fearful; and that early summer Merlin once again had difficulty in walking. It was suggested that the cause was indeed laminitis, and I was advised he should be kept locked in the stable for several weeks.

He did not, in fact, have laminitis, just a pebble trapped in his foot, and I never locked him in the stable. I did, however, take certain steps. Visitors often bring carrots and chocolate biscuits which give the donkeys much delight. I had now to be cruel to be kind. I scrawled a notice on a piece of wood: 'MERLIN AND SUSIE ON A DIET — ALAS NO EXTRAS!'

On the other hand, there have always been some visitors who have arrived without carrots, without chocolate biscuits, and a pantomime thereupon used to take place. The visitors would stand at the gate calling the donkeys, and the donkeys, grazing comfortably in a far part of the field, would look up, then slowly amble over, no doubt expecting a reward for their effort. They would be greeted by words of endearment and admiration, photographs would be taken, Susie would push in front of Merlin, Merlin would try to push her away. Each was trying to be the first to receive the reward. But the reward was not what they expected. The visitors, instead of producing a handful of carrots, a packet of biscuits, would flounder around pulling up grass, picking a campion or a daisy, thrusting these ridiculous presents at the donkey, who would respond with a withering stare.

Sometimes, in a congenial mood, they would escort a visitor around Oliver land. It is one of the special pleasures that I have that I can say to a visitor: 'Go off and wander, take your time, feel . . .' The donkeys would lead them up the field to blackthorn alley, then right along the secret path past the giant badger sett, and on to the Ambrose Rock, and then back by the honeysuckle meadow. The visitors would return with a joyous account of their adventure, or occasionally there was doubt in their tone: 'Susie is a bit boisterous, isn't she? Nearly knocked me over!'

Such incidents softened the other events, the other experiences, from which no one can escape. I may live in surroundings which may be as ideal as I can wish for, but I still have myself to contend with, my dreams, my frustrations, my awareness that my life can never be complete again. All pleasures now are fleeting ones.

Such incidents, because of their simplicity, heighten the horrors that fill our twentieth-century world. While the visitors were being escorted by the donkeys, another vast area of the rain forests was being sawn down, leaving animals, birds and myriad insects bewildered and left to die. For what purpose? Just in order to satisfy the superficial desires of the plastic society. Nor in the West do we behave in better fashion. Daily the green fields of Britain are disappearing, beautiful landscapes destroyed, depriving the birds and animals of their rightful homes. Again for what purpose? Just in order to satisfy the consequence of an overpopulated Britain.

Yesterday I had a musical evening. It had turned cold in June during the day, and I had lit a fire, burning the wood from the dead elm trees. A near gale had sprung up, and it was cosy in the cottage. I had had braised beef cooked in the Prestige pressure cooker with carrots, onion, celery and a dash of red wine. It was delicious. So I settled down to a personal concert. The music I played began with Delius's 'Song of Summer', then followed Brahms's Second Violin Concerto, finishing with Rachmaninov's glorious Second Symphony played by the London Symphony Orchestra conducted by André Previn, and which I made my main choice when I was a castaway on Roy Plomley's *Desert Island Discs*. As the last phrase of the symphony was ending I remembered again the scene when, after lunching at Claridge's with Roy Plomley and his producer Derek Drescher, we were about to set off for the studio and Jeannie hung back. I can see her now.

I continued to sit there on the sofa after the room became silent, and I began thumbing through a notebook of quotations which I had copied out from various sources, years ago, before I was twenty-one. I was fascinated by the maturity of my choices. How did I have the instinct to choose quotations which, as it turned out, were to guide my life?

The quotations suited me at the time. My family life was a very happy one, yet I felt hemmed in by their conventionality. I wanted to break out, but I did not know which way to go, and I did not know whether I was justified in feeling the way I did.

The first quotation comes from George Moore's *Confessions of a Young Man*, a book which greatly influenced me at the time:

> Respectability! . . . a suburban villa, a piano in the drawing room, and going home to dinner. Such things are no doubt very excellent, but they do not promote intensity of feeling, fervour of mind; and as art in itself is an outcry against the normality of human existence, it would be well that the life of the artist should be a practical protest against the so-called decencies of life.

These other two quotations both come from Somerset Maugham's *The Moon and the Sixpence*, the novel based on Gauguin's time in Tahiti. When I was in Tahiti I made a pilgrimage to the site of Gauguin's home, or *faré* as it is called in Tahitian. Nothing much was to be seen, only the atmosphere to feel. I was not alone when I was there. A young American was squatting on his haunches on the outskirts, and I was a little vexed that he was spoiling my wish for solitude.

'What are you doing here?' I asked politely.

'I'm here,' he said, 'because I am a failed artist and I am praying to Gauguin to help me.'

The reason I must have chosen this first of the Somerset Maugham quotations, similar in theme to the one by George Moore, is that I was scared that my life was going to be a dull one.

The story of innumerable couples, and the pattern of life it offers, has a homely grace. It reminds you of a placid rivulet meandering smoothly through green pastures and shaded by pleasant trees, till at last it falls into the sea. But the sea is so calm, so silent, so indifferent, that you are troubled suddenly by a vague uneasiness.

Perhaps it is only a kink in my nature, strong in me even in those days, that I felt in such an existence something amiss. I recognized its social value, I saw its ordered happiness, but a fever in my blood asked for a wilder course. There seemed to me something alarming in such easy delights. In my heart was a desire to live more dangerously. I was not unprepared for jagged rocks and treacherous shoals if I could only have change . . . change and the excitement of the unforeseen.

He would not have written in such placid fashion today although his theme would have been the same. He was then referring to the boredom of a regular, safe existence which trapped people. Today it is financial stress, take-overs, sudden forced change of jobs, endless struggle to keep up with the demands of the plastic society. Nothing has changed except the pace.

The second quotation concerns the appreciation of beauty. I remember that I was fumbling in my mind at the time as to why I did not immediately appreciate certain great pieces of music, and that I did not immediately receive an emotional elation when first looking at a great painting. The quotation helped to make me understand why:

> Why should you think that beauty, which is the most precious thing in the world, lies like a stone on the beach for the careless passers-by to pick up idly? Beauty is something wonderful and strange that the artist fashions out of the chaos of the world in the torment of his soul. And when he has made it, it is not given to all to know it. To recognize it you must repeat the adventure of the artist. It is a melody that he sings to you, and to hear it again in your own heart, you want knowledge, and sensitiveness, and imagination.

I used to read these quotations to girls sitting beside me on the sofa in my cottage in Elm Park Garden Mews near the King's Road in Chelsea. Some looked blank as I read them. Some were alerted. As for myself my philosophy is still the same. I still take risks. I still make mistakes as a consequence. I still pretend that geese can be turned into swans. I am still aware that difference in age is of little consequence, that it is being on the same wavelength that matters. I still despair that those who died in the wars, believing they were protecting the Biritish way of life, protecting their homes, their villages, their streets, died in vain. I still rejoice when I meet someone with whom there is an instant union. I still believe in magic.

Cherry came in and jumped on my lap. I hadn't turned the record player off, and it was humming. I would have liked some more music, but now I could not move.

I continued instead to contemplate, and my contemplation centred around the ink in that old notebook, recording hopes of my future, long before I ever knew Jeannie existed; and my contemplation compared the circumstances of the present.

I have lived on borrowed time since my twenties, all of my generation who survived, have done so. We also belonged to a generation who were not pestered by scientists trying to justify their jobs, and thereby spoiling our enjoyment of life, by issuing sinister warnings as to how and what we should eat, how much we should drink, what exercise we should take, and generally behave ourselves in a strictly orthodox, dull manner. My generation had fun out of being natural, just as it experienced tragedy out of circumstances beyond their control. Yet today there is a growing wave of courageous, persistent, determination to do in peace what our generation did in war.

The goal, this time, is not that of winning a war, but the winning of a green future for all mankind.

As for myself, my personal view of my future has always been a simple one. It is this. The only fear about death is the fear of what happens to the loved one, or the animals, who are left. 'Who will look after them?' is the worry.

Thus, if you die alone, without this fear, you die free.

Cherry was still on my lap, but on this occasion I had no need to be reminded that the evening gull would be waiting as dusk fell. I had kept some tasty left-over scraps for him, and I was looking forward to giving it to him.

'Sorry Cherry,' I said, gently lifting her off my lap.

Then I went outside, and there was the gull, a shadow against the dying light.

'Here you are!' I called out, and then threw him the scraps.

I could now go to bed, my conscience clear.

Mike the postman was earlier than usual the following morning.

'A recorded letter for you to sign,' he said cheerfully.

I signed.

'Another lovely morning,' he said.

I opened the letter.

It was from the Department of the Environment Heritage Division.

Minack had been listed. Minack was now a part of the English Heritage.

JEANNIE
A LOVE STORY

Derek Tangye

When Jeannie and Derek Tangye withdrew to a cliff-top
flower farm in Cornwall, sophisticated London society
protested, but an even wider circle was enriched by the
enchanted life which they shared and which Derek
recorded in the MINACK CHRONICLES. Jeannie died
in 1986, and, in tribute to her extraordinary personality,
her husband has written this portrait of their marriage.
All the delight of the MINACK CHRONICLES is here
– the daffodils, the donkeys and the Cornish magic. And
all the fizzle and pop of champagne days at the Savoy is
captured as Jeannie dazzles admirers from Danny Kaye
to Christian Dior.

GREAT MINACK STORIES

Derek Tangye

Great Minack Stories contains three highly-acclaimed volumes of Derek Tangye's memoirs: *The Way to Minack*, *A Cornish Summer* and *A Cottage on a Cliff*. They combine to tell the unique, touching and highly rewarding story of how he and his wife Jeannie turned an implausible dream into an idyllic reality.

Always yearning to 'get away from it all', Derek and Jeannie left their hectic life in London for the peace and tranquility of a flower farm in Cornwall.

These memoirs highlight the contrasts and trace the pleasures and pitfalls of both ways of life: the fascinating people from the bright lights – Gertrude Lawrence, Alec Waugh, A. P. Herbert, Kim Philby, Harold Macmillan and Aneurin Bevin – and the enchanting Cornish years that brought them closer to nature and to a deeper, lasting joy.

SOMEWHERE A CAT IS WAITING

Derek Tangye

Derek Tangye's fascinating tales of life at Minack, his flower farm on the rugged Cornish coast, are known and loved all over the world. Now three of his most famous books, *A Cat in the Window*, *Lama* and *A Cat Affair* have been revised and abridged to tell the whole enchanting story of the four cats who have shared his idyll.

Beginning with Monty, the lordly ginger tom who, as a kitten, turned Derek Tangye from cat-hater into cat-lover, he progresses to Lama, the little black waif who came to the door of Minack in a storm, and finally to Ambrose and Oliver, the inseparable duo who determined to install themselves firmly in the Tangye's favour. Here, for the first time, the cats of Minack are all together in one volume, superbly illustrated with photographs that show the full beauty of Derek and Jean Tangye's very special country world.

☐	A Gull on the Roof	Derek Tangye	£4.50
☐	A Cat in the Window	Derek Tangye	£4.50
☐	Somewhere a Cat is Waiting	Derek Tangye	£5.99
☐	Jeannie	Derek Tangye	£4.99
☐	The World of Minack	Derek Tangye	£4.99
☐	Monty's Leap	Derek Tangye	£4.99
☐	Great Minack Stories	Derek Tangye	£6.99

Warner Books now offers an exciting range of quality titles by both established and new authors which can be ordered from the following address:

Little, Brown and Company (UK),
P.O. Box 11,
Falmouth,
Cornwall TR10 9EN.

Alternatively you may fax your order to the above address.
Fax No. 01326 317444.

Payments can be made as follows: cheque, postal order (payable to Little, Brown and Company) or by credit cards, Visa/Access. Do not send cash or currency. UK customers and B.F.P.O. please allow £1.00 for postage and packing for the first book, plus 50p for the second book, plus 30p for each additional book up to a maximum charge of £3.00 (7 books plus).

Overseas customers including Ireland, please allow £2.00 for the first book plus £1.00 for the second book, plus 50p for each additional book.

NAME (Block Letters) ....

....

ADDRESS ....

....

....

☐ I enclose my remittance for ....

☐ I wish to pay by Access/Visa Card

Number ☐☐☐☐☐☐☐☐☐☐☐☐☐☐☐☐☐☐

Card Expiry Date ☐☐☐☐